# SUHRAWARDI

# NOTE ON THE ILLUSTRATIONS

The callighraphy "Light upon Light" that appears on the cover and the opposite page is by calligrapher Mohamad Zakariyah, as is the basmalah on the previous page. The other calligraphies of the Beautiful Names of Allah within the text are from the Grand Mosque (Ulu Cami) built in 1399 in Bursa, Turkey. The originals are monumental mural compositions of calligraphy approximately eight feet in height, painted in the nineteenth century by the world-renowned calligrapher Mehmet Shefik.

# SUHRAWARDI
## The Shape of Light

*Hayakal al-Nur*

Hazrat Shihabuddin Yahya al-Suhrawardi

*Interpreted by*
*Shaykh Tosun Bayrak al-Jerrahi al-Halveti*

FONS VITAE

First published in 1998 by Fons Vitae
49 Mockingbird Valley Drive
Louisville, KY 40207
email: fonsvitaeky@aol.com
website: www.fonsvitae.com

Second Printing, 2006

Library of Congress
Catalog Card Number: 98-73351

ISBN: 1-887752-15-3

Printed in Canada by Friesens through
Four Colour Imports Ltd. Louisville, KY

# CONTENTS

# LIST OF ILLUSTRATIONS

Allah is the Light
of the heavens and the earth;
the likeness of His Light is as a niche
wherein is a lamp — the lamp in a glass,
the glass as it were a brightly shining star
kindled from a blessed Olive Tree
that is neither of the East nor of the West,
whose oil well-nigh would shine,
though fire does not touch it;
Light upon Light;
Allah guides to His Light
whom He wills.

(*Nur*, 35)

# AN ADDRESS TO THE READER

Dear friend, your heart is a polished mirror. You must wipe it clean of the veil of dust which has gathered upon it, because it is destined to reflect the light of divine secrets. When the light from

> Allah [Who] is the Light
> of the heavens and the earth

starts shining upon the regions of your heart, the lamp of the heart will be lit. The lamp of the heart

> is in a glass, the glass is as it were
> a brightly shining star

Then within that heart, the lightning of divine discoveries strikes. This lightning will generate from the thunder-clouds of meaning

> neither of the East nor of the West,
> kindled from a blessed olive tree

and shedding light upon the tree of discovery, so pure, so transparent that it

> shines though fire does not touch it.
> (*Nur*, 35)

Then the lamp of wisdom is lit by itself. How can it remain unlit when the light of Allah's secrets shines over it? If

9

only the light of divine secrets shines upon it, the night sky of secrets will be lit with thousands of stars,

> and by the stars [you] find [your] way
> (*Nahl*, 16)

It is not the stars that guide us, but the divine light. For Allah has

> decked the lower heaven
> with beauty [in] the stars.
> (*Ya Sin*, 6)

If only the lamp of divine secrets is kindled in your inner self, the rest will come, either all at once or little by little. Some you already know, some we will tell you here. Read, listen, try to understand. The dark skies of unconsciousness will be lit by divine presence and the peace and beauty of the full moon, which will rise from the horizon shedding

> Light upon Light
> (*Nur*, 35)

ever rising in the sky, passing through its appointed stage as Allah has

> ordained for it stages, till it
> (*Ya Sin*, 39)

shines in glory in the center of the sky, dispersing the darkness of heedlessness.

(I swear) by the night when it is still,
*(Dhuha*, 2)

By the glorious morning light,
*(Dhuha*, 1)

your night of unconsciousness will see the brightness of the
day. Then you will inhale the perfume of remembrance and

repent in the early hours of the morning
*(Al-i 'Imran*, 17)

of unconsciousness, and regret your life spent in sleep.
You will hear the songs of the morning nightingales, and
you will hear them say

They were in the habit of sleeping but little
by night, and in the hours of early dawn,
[they were found] praying for forgiveness.
*(Zariyat*, 17-18)

Allah guides to His Light Whom He pleases.
*(Nur*, 35)

Then you will see from the horizon of Divine Reason the
sun of inner knowledge rising. It is your private sun, for
you are the one

whom Allah guides,

and are

on the right path,

and not the one

He leaves in error.
*(Araf,* 178)

And you will understand the secret that

It is not permitted to the sun to catch up
to the moon, nor can the night outstrip the day.
Each swims along in (its appointed) orbit.
*(Ya Sin,* 40)

Finally, the knot will be untied in accordance with

the parables which Allah sets forth for men,
and Allah is knower of all things,
*(Nur,* 35)

and the veils will lift and shells will shatter, showing the fine under the coarse; the truth will uncover her face. All this will start when the mirror of your heart is cleansed. The light of the divine secrets will fall upon it if you wish and ask for Him, from Him, with Him.

—FROM A LETTER BY HADRAT ʿABDUL-QADIR AL-JILANI

# INTERPRETER'S INTRODUCTION

# *Mystical Philosophy versus the Philosophy of Sufism*

To explain the point of view of Suhrawardi in this work, it is necessary to clarify the difference between two approaches which, while resembling each other in some ways, are nonetheless distinct: one is generally known as mystical philosophy, and the other may be called the philosophy of Sufism.

Mystical philosophy is a system of thought built upon the theory of acquiring knowledge through inspiration and revelation, and devoting itself to the exploration of mysteries. In the Islamic world at the time of Suhrawardi, this type of philosophy was called *ishraqiyyah* (philosophy of illumination; literally illumination by the pure light devoid of matter, from the Orient [*sharq*] of the soul).

*Ishraqiyyah* is, in a sense, metaphysics of light. Although consideration of light versus darkness has been the basis of many other philosophies and religions, particularly Zoroastrianism, with which *ishraqi* philosophers may have been conversant, the mystical philosophers of the *ishraqiyyah* were not by any means dissociated from Islamic orthodoxy (*shari'ah*). On the contrary, they reconciled orthodoxy with their philosophy, and combined the two. They tried to explain their philosophy by Islam and

Islam by their philosophy. *Ishraqiyyah* takes the Qur'an as its witness:

> Allah is the Protector of those who have faith;
> from the depths of darkness
> He will lead them forth to light.
> The evil ones are the patrons
> of those who reject faith.
> From light they will lead them
> into the depths of darkness.
> They will be companions of the Fire,
> dwelling therein [forever].
> (*Baqarah*, 257)

> There hath come to you from Allah
> a [new] light and a clear Book,
> Wherewith Allah guideth all who seek
> His good pleasure to ways of peace and safety
> and leadeth them out of darkness,
> by His Will, unto the light
> guideth them to a path that is straight.
> (*Ma'idah*, 15-16)

Joining Qur'anic teaching with the influence of the newly rediscovered and translated works of the Greek philosophers culminating in Plato, many Muslim sages known to the West—such as Ibn Sina, Halabi, and to a certain extent al-Farabi—pursued the philosophy of visionary intuition.

Mystical *ishraqi* philosophy was not the only type of philosophy known to the Islamic world. Another trend called *mashshiyyah* (Peripateticism), under the influence of the rationalistic philosophy of Aristotle, was earlier adapted by Ibn Rushd (Averroes), Ibn Tufayl, Ibn Bajjah, and others in Islamic Spain. This Islamic Aristotelianism of Ibn Rushd was translated into Latin and had a great influence on Christian thought, destroying Augustinian mysticism and leading the way to the rationalism and naturalism of the Renaissance.

Suhrawardi's doctrines replaced the earlier direct influences of Aristotelian rationalism and Platonic intuitivism. Suhrawardi, who entered upon the Sufi path and engaged in its spiritual practices of retreat and meditation, is also considered to be the principal propagator of the doctrine of *ishraqiyyah*. Yet he is not a mystical philosopher in the ordinary sense, but a philosopher of Sufism. Sufi philosophers, like others, contemplate the value of thought, the source of eternal truth and the reason for man's being. However, in Sufism this search is made actively rather than intellectually. This action may take several forms.

One sort, which encompasses all aspects of living, is the effort to apply devotion, moral codes, consciousness, and conscience to every instant of one's daily life. This requires constant evaluation and attempt at improvement. Such an active spiritual search results in an accumulation of experiences and of knowledge gathered through these conscious personal experiences. The resulting wisdom is called *ma'rifah*, the inner wisdom, philosophy of being and action impervious to the influences of other philosophies due to its subjective nature.

Or the Sufi may go into *khalwah*, seclusion. Retired from the world, he meditates upon Allah, man, and the creation, and comes to a conclusion. The outcome of this meditative experience cannot relate to any other school of thought.

Or by pious asceticism, prayers, concerted efforts, and the mortification of his flesh, the Sufi receives revelations and observes phenomena invisible to others. This also is a knowledge which does not fit into another category of philosophy.

Thus there are two sides to Sufism: knowledge and action. Devotion, obedience to Allah, fear and love of Allah, abstention from the unlawful, and *adab* (perfected behavior and morals) are all in the realm of action. This is the point of departure of Sufism. Spiritual knowledge, wisdom, inspiration, the opening of the inner meaning and the divine mysteries, and finally Truth—are in the realm of knowledge. This is the purpose of Sufism.

With piety, asceticism, and meditation, the Sufi hopes to cleanse his heart and achieve an inner order. This in turn brings his soul to an inspired state of wisdom. Action is the cause and knowledge is the effect. Piety, asceticism, and perfect behavior are the means; knowledge is the result. This knowledge cannot be attained either by reflection or by reasoning. It can only be given as a gift by Allah through revelation. There cannot be a Sufism which depends upon knowledge without action. Neither does a life of piety and asceticism which does not attain wisdom become Sufism.

Knowledge of this sort, attained by these methods, when put forth in explicit terms may be called the philosophy of Sufism. The nature of this knowledge gives to this philosophy a status different from any other. Many Sufi saints and sages such as Sulami, Qushayri, Kalabadhi, 'Abdul-Qadir al-Jilani, Junayd al-Baghdadi, and Mawlana Jalaluddin Rumi (may their souls be sanctified) in their lives, in their teachings and writings, have demonstrated and confirmed this philosophy manifested in their own and each other's spiritual experiences. In their expositions, these saints relate their personal spiritual experiences and explain on a higher level of understanding the orthodox Islamic theology of scripture, dogma, doctrines, and canon.

At the time of Suhrawardi there seemed to exist four principal paths to spiritual knowledge, divine truth, and salvation. As the realm of intellectual reflection contained the visionary philosophy of the *ishraqiyyah* and the rationalist arguments of the *mashshiyyah*, so the realm of scriptural interpretation included the intuitive application of the Sufis and the logical inferences of the Islamic scholasticism known as *kalam*. According to this classification, those who follow the exegesis of *kalam* hold reliance on the dogma in common with the Sufis, and share rationalism with the Aristotelian philosophers of the *mashshiyyah*. The Sufis, sharing dependence on the scriptures with the scholastics of the *kalam*, as mentioned, have their method of intuitionism in common with the Platonic philosophers of the *ishraqiyyah*.

Tradition divides the spirituals into two categories: *ahl al-nazar*, the speculatives, and *ahl al-riyadat*, the practitioners of spiritual experience. The speculatives, if they assign final authority to the canons of Islam, belong to the followers of *kalam*. If they do not, they are philosophers of the *mashshiyyah*. The practitioners of spiritual experience, if they measure experience against the canons of Islam, are called Sufis; if they do not, they are philosophers of the *ishraqiyyah*.

In practice, this categorical division was not so rigid. The Aristotelian *mashshiyyah*, claiming that an unadulterated pure reason is able to solve every problem and answer all questions, and the Neoplatonic *ishraqiyyah*, based on the idea that everything can be explained and evaluated by individual inspiration, are both philosophically independent of religious dogma; the role that transmitted teaching actually plays in them varies with the philosopher. Likewise, the degree of rationalism in *kalam* and the degree of intuitionism in Sufism—both of which depend ultimately on scripture—are variable and not constant. It all depends upon the personality of the sage. For instance, among scholastics, Fakhr al-Razi gives more authority to the faculty of reason than does Abduh al-Maali; among Sufis, the saint Mawlana Jalaluddin Rumi and the order of the Mawlawiyyah rely less strictly upon doctrinal principles than do the saint Baha'uddin Naqshbandi and the order of the Naqshbandiyyah. Thus there was often no definite border between the scholasticism of *kalam* and the rationalism of the *mashshiyyah*, nor between the intuitionism of the philosophy of *ishraqiyyah* and the personal inspirations of the Sufis. It can be a very nebulous boundary. A Sufi, without realizing it, may pass to the ranks of the Neoplatonic philosophy of the *ishraqiyyah*, and a sect depending on the local argument of *kalam* may find itself participating in the Aristotelian rationalism of the *mashshiyyah*. There has always been a conflict between the religious scholasticism of *kalam* and the Sufis. The theosophers of *kalam*, in their attacks on Sufism, leaned upon the rationalist philosophy, while the Sufis, when they reproached the philosophers of *kalam*, supported their arguments with the point of view and the proofs of the intuitive, visionary philosophy of *ishraqiyyah*.

This relationship with the philosophies corresponding to their beliefs, used by the Sufis and the theosophers of *kalam* in their attacks upon each other, led them to call each other *zindiq*, those who distort religion with the influence of non-Islamic sources. This conflict is confined only to the theosophers of *kalam* who give priority to rationalism over the dogma, and to the Sufis who give priority to visionary intuition over the dogma. *Kalam* and Sufism which conform with the tenets of Islam rather than those of the philosophers can coexist in perfect harmony. The best example of this is al-Ghazali, whose rational argument was responsible for breaking the power of Aristotelian rationalism and destroying tenets of philosophy in general which were contrary to Islamic teaching.

When the majesty of the transmission is uppermost, petty quarrels based on differences of opinion lose their force. The great Sufi Sari al-Saqati has said, "The light of wisdom in a Sufi does not put out the light of the fear of Allah in him. The inner knowledge which he possesses cannot contradict the open meaning of the Qur'an and the hadith. The miracles which he performs cannot tear the veils of the secrecy of Allah."

Like al-Ghazali, Suhrawardi investigated all the modes of knowledge available to his time, and finally put this vast experience to work in the service of Sufism, opening the inner meaning of Islam. Suhrawardi declared in relation to this work, "Although before the composition of this book, I composed several summary treatises on Aristotelian philosophy, this book differs from them and has a method peculiar to itself. All of its material has been assembled not by thought and reasoning, but rather by intuition, contemplation, and ascetic practices."[1]

---

1. Suhrawardi, *Opera*, ed. Henri Corbin (II.10.11)

The Messenger of Allah (ﷺ)[2] has related a *hadith qudsi*, or non-Qur'anic divine utterance, in which Allah says,

> When I love My servant, I am his eye,
> so that he sees by Me.
> I am his ear, so that he hears by Me.
> I am his tongue, so that he speaks by Me.
> I am his hand, so that he takes by Me.

This state is the state of annihilation of one's will and materiality in Allah. Suhrawardi was in that state.

Such a condition opens possibilities of perception not available to humanity in ordinary circumstances. Suhrawardi sees the image of Light by a particular mode of perception unlike the sensory experience, very much like the imagination.

A rational person knows that the things ordinarily imagined are unreal, nonfactual inventions of the mind. On the other hand we know that there are real yet invisible forces which express themselves in invisible shapes and phenomena. Man possesses the faculty of observing the cause, the reason, the essence, the finer reality of the coarse reality which the senses observe, as well as celestial realities which do not have their corresponding coarse worldly realities. In a way, the sensory reality has become a veil between us and the Real reality. True inner perception is not something derived from any outer perception, as

---

2. ﷺ or "s.a.w.s." indicates *salla Allahu 'alayhi wa sallam*, "may Allah's peace and blessings be upon him," a prayer which always attends the mention of the name of the Prophet.

is ordinary imagination, which simply reshuffles impressions and is as limited as the senses. Rather it is seeing the inner image directly through the inner eye, or *basirah*.

As the coarse worldly image appears on the retina of the physical eye, the inner image is reflected on the pure mirror of the cleansed heart as a transparent spiritual form of light, and is imprinted on the soul itself. As the mortal body observes and feeds upon temporal things and experiences, the immortal soul sees and relates to the essence of things. This perception is the soul's cognizance of itself.

Saints who see with the eyes of Allah and speak with the tongue of Allah sometimes make powerful declarations like the famous *ana al-haqq* ("I am the Truth") or *Subhani* ("Glory to Me"). At such times, names attributed to Allah alone come from the lips of an al-Hallaj or a Beyazid without their will. The Sufi writer Qushayri reproaches such sages and says, "Sufis sometimes make statements whose meanings are known to themselves but which are totally unable to be understood by others."

The danger of misunderstanding is very great. Hallaj declared, "I witness God, I am unified with Him"; others understood him to say "I am God," and he was martyred. The case of Suhrawardi was the same.

The subject of Sufism is the soul. The Sufis use the terms *latifah* (grace); *sirr* (secret soul); *nafs* (essence); *qalb* (heart or center); and others. All essentially mean the soul. Purification of the soul, cleansing of the heart, to put one's essence in perfect order, to be centered, and to be one are the goals of Sufism. The one who can actualize this is the perfect man.

Previously we have spoken of Sufi philosophy. As the purpose and the subject of Sufism is the soul, then in a sense Sufism is also psychology. Knowledge, emotions, motivation, and action are the principal subjects of both Sufism and psychology. Psychology, which claims to be positive, stays within the boundaries of measures, experimentation, and measurable experiences. Sufism, although seemingly confined by the principles of Islam, includes knowledge received in states of ecstasy, rapture, and divine love, which surpasses the limits of logic and measurement.

Morals — right and wrong in the context of divine judgment — are not usually included within the goals of psychology. In Sufism, however, the religious states and revelations and their resulting knowledge depend on the application of the objective standards of the dogma and the canon to one's intentions and one's deeds. The example of the Prophet (ﷺ) and the saints and sages as teachers and perfect men are followed toward this end. From this perspective, Sufism is also pedagogy. This education of the soul is expressed in the words *akhlaq*, morals; and *adab*, the perfect manner of behavior.

There are three aspects to man:

1. *Khuluq, akhlaq* (disposition): one's nature and potential as existent at birth. This disposition, if it is not in accordance with what is lawful and desirable according to divine judgment, can be ameliorated by continuous and organized effort—*mujahadah*, struggle.

2. *Fi'l* (deed): willful actions such as pious devotion, obedience and submission to religious prescriptions, and good works.

3. *Hal, ahwal* (state): states which come to one without one's will. The beneficence and purity of these states correspond to the purity of one's disposition and one's deeds. These states are of two kinds:

- States of *wajd*, exaltation; *jadhbah*, ecstasy; *sukr*, spiritual intoxication; *istighraq*, trance; *qabd*, contraction; *bast*, expansion, etc. These are higher emotional states.

- *Ilham*, inspiration; *firasah*, intuition; *kashf*, discovery; *yaqin*, certitude; *haqq*, truth; *'irfan*, refined knowledge; *ma'rifah*, the inner wisdom. These are the intellectual, intuitive and visionary states which lead to wisdom.

These three aspects interact in the following way: Man prays with his will, lives a pious life, does good deeds according to what is lawful, and avoids what is unlawful; this changes his negative dispositions and opens him to receiving mystical states of exaltation and ecstasy; through these states he obtains the inspiration, the discovery, and the certitude of inner wisdom.

Thus mystical states depend on one's disposition and one's disposition is ameliorated by one's willful good deeds; refined inner knowledge is the reward for these deeds. *Akhlaq*, the disposition, and *fi'l*, the willful good deeds, are in the realm of the *shari'ah*, Islamic dogma. *Hal*, beatific state, the source of wisdom, falls within the realm of Sufism. Since *hal*, the higher state, depends upon *akhlaq*, disposition, and *fi'l*, action, Islam is the foundation, and Sufism is the house built upon it.

A house cannot be built without foundations. A foundation can exist without a house built upon it, yet the purpose of a foundation is to have a house built upon it. Islamic dogma is the body, Sufism is the soul. The religion is the word, Sufism is the meaning. The dogma is the sea, Sufism is the pearl in the sea. The religion is milk, Sufism is its cream. The religion is the tree, Sufism is its fruit. Islam is the shape of light, and Sufism is the light within that shape.

Allah is the Light
of the heavens and the earth;
the likeness of His Light is as a niche
wherein is a lamp — the lamp in a glass,
the glass as it were a brightly shining star
kindled from a blessed olive tree
that is neither of the East nor of the West,
whose oil well-nigh would shine,
though fire does not touch it;
Light upon Light;
Allah guides to His Light
whom He wills.
(*Nur*, 35)

Allah, may His glory be exalted. (Allah, the word of glory [*lafz al-jalal*] is the personal name [*ism al-dhat*]of God, the name of His essence and His totality. It is written with four letters. When the initial letter, *alif* is removed, the three remaining letters are the symbol of the universe, of existence, which consists of the visible world [*dunya*] and the invisible heavens above the starry firmament; purgatory [*barzakh*] and heaven; the hereafter [*akhira*]. The first letter, *alif*, is the source of all, and the last letter, *hu* [He], is Allah's most perfect attribute free from all associations.)

# ON SUHRAWARDI

Suhrawardi was born in 549 A.H. (1155 A.D.) in the town of Suhraward in the province of Jabal in Azerbaijan. In the city of Maraghah in Azerbaijan he studied Islamic law and theosophy under Shaykh Majduddin al-Jili. Later he traveled to Isfahan, then a leading center of learning in Persia, and completed his education under Zahiruddin al-Qari'.

As a young man he was well known as a theosopher, theologian, and doctor of Islamic law. He traveled widely in the provinces of the Seljuk Empire, in Persia, in Anatolia, and in Syria. During these travels he met many Sufi masters and became strongly attached to them; he entered upon the Sufi path and practiced for long periods of time pious devotion, spiritual retreats, and meditation. During his travels he visited Harran, Antalya, Nusaybin, and Urfa in Northern Syria, a region which was the cultural center of Hermeticism before the advent of Islam. It is possible that some of the thoughts from that source which appear in Suhrawardi's theosophy came through his contacts during these travels. Finally he was invited by Malik Zahir, the governor of Aleppo, to settle in that city. Zahir was the son of the famous victor of the Crusades, Salahuddin al-Ayyubi. He became the patron of Suhrawardi, and often invited him to his palace for discourses with other wise men of the period.

Suhrawardi had an extraordinary intelligence in addition to the esoteric wisdom he had received through his teachers and the direct inspiration granted him through his Sufi practices. This enabled him to overcome all opponents in those debates. He was fearless and outspoken, which made him many enemies.

Many orthodox authorities—especially the doctors of law—claimed that he was propagating doctrines against the tenets of the faith; his knowledge of alchemy made Suhrawardi appear to them as a sorcerer. They subsequently asked for his execution. In fact, there is a tradition according to which Malik Zahir asked Suhrawardi one day to show him an example of his knowledge of alchemy. Although Suhrawardi at first refused, claiming that such practice was not for the eyes and comprehension of the governor, he conceded upon his patron's insistence.

After certain preparations and recitations, he asked the governor to come to the balcony of the palace and look at the walls of the city. The whole city was surrounded by Mongol armies attacking the walls! Soon the walls were swarming with them, and they were killing and destroying everything in front of them. They were coming toward the palace from all directions. Finally when they reached the gates of the palace, Malik Zahir, in terror, wanting to take refuge, rushed to the *harem*. Opening the door of the *harem*, he came face to face with a seven-headed dragon. He fell down and fainted.

Suhrawardi brought him back, took him to the balcony, and showed him the city of Aleppo, peaceful and beautiful, shining under the sun. It is said that this incident brought the change of heart to Suhrawardi's patron.

Suhrawardi's enemies finally went to Salahuddin Ayyubi to convince him that this sorcerer was a danger to the religion and to the country. Syria had just been recaptured from the Crusaders, and Salahuddin needed the support of the doctors of law to maintain his authority. This political consideration was the reason for his ordering Malik Zahir to imprison and execute Suhrawardi.[1]

According to another tradition, Malik Zahir accepted the wish of Suhrawardi to end his life by total fasting rather than being put to death by execution. Thus Suhrawardi left this world and met his Lord in the year 587 A.H. (1191 A.D.) at the age of thirty-eight, by the Sufi practice of mortification of the flesh through total fasting.

Despite his short life, Suhrawardi wrote nearly fifty books, both in Arabic and Persian, most of which have been translated into other languages in Islamic countries. Among the most important are:[2]

1. *Hikmat al-ishraq* (The Theosophy of Illumination), which is considered his masterpiece and became the basis of the theosophy of the ishraqiyya. This work has been printed in Shiraz, Iran, with a fourteenth century commentary by Mahmud ibn Mas 'ud al-Shirazi.

2. *Kitab al-talwihat al-lawiyyah wal-'arshiyyah* (The Book of Allusions to Allah's Secrets and His Throne).

3. *Kitab al-muqawamat* (The Book of Oppositions).

4. *Kitab al-mashari wal-mutarahat* (The Book of Paths and Conversations).

---

1. See the chapter on the ideas and writings of Suhrawardi in Seyyed Hossein Nasr's *Three Muslim Sages* (Cambridge, Harvard University Press, 1964). pp. 52–82.
2. Ibid., pp. 58—59.

(The last three, dealing with modifications of Aristotelian philosophy, were published by Henri Corbin under the title *Majmu'ah fil-hikmat al-ilahiyyah.* [Istanbul, 1945])

5. *Hayakal al-nur* (The Shape of Light), the present work, originally written in Arabic but also existing in Persian, was first translated into Turkish in the seventeenth century by Ismail Ankaravi, then by Yusuf Ziya in 1924, and in 1960 by Saffet Yetkin. These Turkish translations are being taken as the basis of this interpretation.

6. *Kitab al-lamahat fil-haqa'iq* (Flashes of Lights of Truths), a book on physics, metaphysics, and logic.

7. *Al-alwah al-'imadiyyah* (Tablets for 'Imaduddin), A book on the philosophy of illumination.

8. *Fi I'tiqad al-hukama'*, (On the Faith of the Philosophers).

9. *Yazdan shinakht* (On the Knowledge of Allah). (in Persian)

10. *Bustan al-qulub* (The Garden of Hearts).

There are other works, mystical novels, depicting the journey of the soul through the realm of Light, containing much of Sufi thought and practices of purification. Most of them are in Persian and a few are in Arabic.

11. *Aql-i surkh* (The Red Archangel; literally, The Red Intellect).

12. *Aswat al-ajnihati Jibra'il* (Sound of the Wings of Gabriel).

13. *Al-ghurbat al-gharbiyyah* (The Occidental Exile).

14. *Lughat-i muran* (The Language of Termites).

15. *Risalah fi halat al-tifuliyyah* (Treatise on the Conditions of Childhood).

16. *Ruzi ba jama'at-i Sufiyan* (A Day with the Community of Sufis).

17. *Risalah fil-mi'raj* (Treatise on the Ascension of the Prophet).

18. *Safir-i simurgh* (The Griffin's Song).

There are other works, translations and commentaries on philosophy, such as the translations and commentaries of Ibn Sina (Avicenna).

19. *Risalat al-tair* (Treatise on Spiritual Flight), a translation.

20. *Isharat* (Advice), a commentary.

21. *Risalah fi haqiqat al-'ishq* (Treatise on the Realities of Love), based on Ibn Sina's *Risalah fil-'ishq*.

There are still other works of commentary on Qur'anic verses and hadith, or Prophetic traditions, and volumes of prayers and supplications.

In all these works shines a wisdom which reflects the lights of many traditions. Plato, Aristotle, Empedocles,

Pythagoras, Plotinus—all of the West—are dissolved in Islam. In the work of Suhrawardi, Plotinus's theory of emanation becomes the flowing of the sacred Light. The idea Plotinus obtained through intuition was the Light of Lights; this was the sacred secret obtained by Suhrawardi through spiritual purification.

The accumulated teachings of Hermeticism, the wisdom and laws of Hermes, who was believed variously to be an alchemist of ancient Egypt whose wisdom was kept by the Sabii of Harran; or the Prophet Idris, founder of philosophy and the sciences; or the line of Persian priest–kings, Gayumarth, Faridun, Kai Khusraw—all converged in the universal wisdom of Suhrawardi. But above all, the precursors of Suhrawardi were the early exemplars of Islamic Sufism: Abu Yazid al-Bistami (d. 261/874), Mansur al-Hallaj (d. 309/992), Dhul Nun al-Misri (d. 245/859), and Sahl al-Tustari (d. 283/896). Suhrawardi himself considered that his most immediate predecessors were these early Sufis. He writes of a dream in which he saw someone he thought to be Aristotle, and asked him if Peripatetic philosophers like al-Farabi and Ibn Sina were the real philosophers in Islam. The Greek philosopher answered, "Not a degree in a thousand. Rather the Sufis Bistami and Tustari are the real philosophers."[3]

Al-Ghazali (d. 505/1111), the catalyst of Sufism and Islamic orthodoxy, also influenced Suhrawardi. His views in *Mishkat al-anwar* (The Niche of Lights), when compared to certain concepts of the theosophy of the *ishraqiyyah*, show this influence. The image demonstrating that all

---

3. Ibid. pp. 61–62.

things come from Allah as light waves spread from the sun is common to both al-Ghazali and Suhrawardi. Al Ghazali in his *al-Risalat al-laduniyyah* (Treatises on the Divine Nature) shows that the consciousness of God and the knowledge of the Divine secrets are only possible through Sufic practices of purification. The same argument appears in Suhrawardi's *Risalat al-tair* (Treatise on Spiritual Flight), *Munis al- 'ushshaq* (Intimate of Lovers), and *Aswat al-ajnihati Jibra'il* (Sounds of the Wings of Gabriel).

Suhrawardi believed in creation through *sudur*, emanation, from one central source: Allah. He is the First, the Light of Lights, the *wajib*, or preexistent absolute necessity, the principal cause upon which all that is *mumkin*, all the possibilities of creation, depend for their existence. This Light of Lights illuminates all things, and is reflected upon all things: upon the suns in the skies, upon the fire in the elements, and upon the soul in man. The creation emanates from Allah, the Light of Lights, as the rays of light shine from the sun and make all visible.

The first created being is also a light, a conscious light, a unique and unified light, immaterial, devoid of multiplicity, a light which knows itself, and knows the Cause of its creation. It is the essential intelligence, the total mind, the intermediary and the intercessor between the source of light, the Creator, and the created universe. This is *al-nur al-Muhammadi*, the Light of Muhammad, which Suhrawardi calls in our book *al-nur al-ibda'i*, the Creative Light; in his *Hikmat al-ishraq* he calls it *al-nur al-aqrab*, the Nearest Light (to its Source). In his *Talwihat* he calls it *al-'aql al-kulli*, the Total Mind. In other books, reference is made to *al-nur al-awwal*, the first Light, *al-shaykh*, the Teacher, *al-jamal*, Beauty, and so on. The reason one thing is given so many different names is Suhrawardi's wish to explain the *nur Muhammadi* in terms of every possible mode of thought and philosophy, whether in adherence to *kalam* or *mashshiyyah* or the philosophy of Plotinus or Aristotle. This First Created Light is different from the Light of Lights in the degree of strength of its light. Every essence of light has a weaker light than that which precedes it, just as the light of the moon is weaker than that of the sun, from which it receives its light. As the light pours continuously from the sun, the creation is continuous from the Light of Lights. As the cause is endless, the effect is endless. As the Creator is eternal, that which comes from It is eternal. Existence is the best and the most beneficent. It cannot be any more perfect. Whatever exists is the best and most beautiful existence. There is no ugliness or badness in the universe, as all is a reflection of Allah.

To attain the realization of the Divine Light in him, man must wage a spiritual battle with himself. The desires of the flesh are the adversaries preventing one from enlightenment. Man has to rid himself of the darkness of the flesh and materialism to reach the Light of Truth. Discipline, contemplation, prayer and devotion are the actions for the cleansing of the heart. Suhrawardi, who follows and professes this path, also insists on the necessity of a guide and a teacher, whose life is for Allah's sake and Allah's pleasure.

Suhrawardi claims that those who devote their lives to the service of Allah will receive secret knowledge, and will attain the power of sanctity, and may work miracles. The best of these miracles are various forms of light which manifest themselves to the seeker. There are various degrees of the revelations of these lights:

1. Quick, lightning-like flashes, which appear and disappear, obtained by novices.

2. More continuous periods of enlightenment, which may become permanent, for those who are continuous and persistent in their efforts, contemplation, and prayers.

3. Revealing lights for those who are advanced in the true path, for whom the struggle with the ego, contemplation and consciousness of the Creator, and devotions have become a natural faculty.

With these spiritual efforts, man can be elevated to the level of annihilation, leaving the material tastes of the world, the flesh, and worldly knowledge, cutting all relationship with the exterior. That is when the soul becomes a mirror upon which Allah's light reflects, and the soul sees the images of Light.

# THE SHAPE
# OF LIGHT

*Hayakal al-Nur*

Hazrat Shihabuddin Yahya al-Suhrawardi

*Interpreted by*
*Shaykh Tosun Bayrak al-Jerrahi al-Halveti*

# INTRODUCTION

*Bismillah al-rahman al-rahim.*

I begin in the Name of Allah, the Beneficent, the Compassionate.

A ll the holy mysteries — Allah's words addressed to men in the one hundred tablets of early scripture, the Psalms of David, the Torah, and the Gospels — are contained within the Qur'an. The whole of the Holy Qur'an is contained within the Surah *al-Fatihah*, the Opening Chapter:

> In the Name of Allah,
> the Beneficent, the Compassionate.
> Praise be to Allah, the Lord of the Worlds,
> the Beneficent, the Compassionate,
> Master of the Day of Judgment.
> You do we worship and
> Your aid do we seek.
> Show us the straight path,
> the path of those on whom
> You have bestowed Your grace,
> those who go not astray,
> and do not receive Your wrath.

The whole of the *Fatihah* is contained in the beginning line,

> In the Name of Allah,
> the Beneficent, the Compassionate,

and the essence of everything is contained in the beginning of the beginning, the first letter, the "B", which contains the secret of

> *bi kana ma kana wa bi yakunu ma yakunu,*
> Whatever became, became through Me,
> and whatever will become,
> will become through Me.

The essence of the essence is in the dot under the letter
"B" ( ﺏ ).

The Prophet Muhammad (ﷺ) said, *Ana madinat al-
'ilm wa 'Ali babuha,* "I am the city of knowledge and 'Ali
(r. a. a.)[3] is the gate to it." 'Ali, that door of wisdom, con-
firms this, saying: "I am the dot under the 'B' ," and *al-
'ilmu nuqtatun,* "all knowledge is a dot."

O *Qayyum,* O Allah, the Self-Existent, on Whom all
existence depends, strengthen us with Your Light, that
pure intelligence free of all imagination, and cover us
with Your Light, that true knowledge reflected in our
actions. Lead us to Your Sacred Light which is Your
Essence.

Let the final goal of all our wishes be Your pleasure,
and let our last wish be to come to You with the perfect
faith and the perfect light which come from You. We have
tyrannized ourselves; and enclosed ourselves in darkness,
yet You have not kept our enlightenment from us. We are
slaves, chained in this dark prison of matter. We are wait-

---

3. "r.a.a." stands for *radiya Allahu 'anhu,* "May Allah Be pleased
with him," a blessing customarily attached to the names of the Prophet's
Companions.

ing at Your door, begging for Your mercy and the good which will come from You to save us.

Good coming from You is Your pleasure; bad coming from You is Your decree. You are mighty and all-existent; You shed enlightenment and mercy upon all existence. Even those of us who take this world and our temporal selves as a god do not draw Your revenge and wrath. Bless us with the wisdom to remember and praise You. Lift the veils of ignorance from between us. Give the righteous the rewards of their hopes. May Your blessing be showered upon the Prophet (ﷺ) and his progeny.

This work is called *Hayakal al-nur*, the shapes, the forms, the appearances, the edifices of Light. As the Greeks of old saw the stars as the material bodies of spiritual existences, these shapes of Light are the manifestation of the source of all light, the Sacred Light.

May the souls of those who lead men to Truth, the men who have the birthright to tread the true path, be sanctified. The true path, the true faith, is that which has been proven by the witnesses of Allah—the prophets, and their inheritors, the beloved lovers of Allah—the saints.

Light upon light
Allah guides to His light
whom He pleases.
(*Nur*, 35)

# THE FIRST FORM OF LIGHT

# *Enlightened Matter*

Matter encompasses everything which depends on perception by the senses for its existence. In all cases, it has length, width, and depth. These characteristics must be noted in order to guard against confusion concerning matter. It is important to realize that the intelligence and the soul, which are invisible, are dependent on matter for their perceptible manifestation. Matter enlightened by intelligence and the soul may point to its essence.

We live in the realm of perception, of our senses. Our material self is of this realm. This world of the senses is in contraposition to the world of *Malakut*—the spiritual kingdom of Allah—which comprises the invisible, the spiritual, incorporeal beings, and abstractions. The key to the wisdom of inner meaning is in the knowledge and ability to distinguish the material world from the spiritual world.

What is common to and creates a unity among material things is that they are all matter. Yet two things which have one common characteristic may differ from one another in other aspects. In the case of material things, the qualities which separate one from the other are in their visual shapes. Otherwise, a thing which is a part of the absolute Truth cannot be other than the Truth.

By definition, the number four is an even number, which relates it to all other even numbers; and the material body defines the human being, relating it to all other human beings. These properties seem to be necessary for the existence of material things. These common qualities in material things may either be an absolute necessity for their existence, *wajib*; or possible, *mumkin* (i.e., in some cases necessary, in others not); or impossible, *mumtani'*, negating their existence. For instance, it is an absolute necessity for a human being to possess a material body, it is possible for a man to stand up or sit down, and it is impossible for him to be a horse!

*Wajib*, *mumkin*, and *mumtani'* are terms pertaining to the science of inner meaning. *Wajib* means an absolute necessity. *Mumkin* is a possibility whose chance of being or not being is equal. *Mumtani'* is an impossibility whose not being is an absolute necessity.

It is not right to suppose that a thing or a concept which is absolutely indivisible can exist in a defined space. The smallest matter which defies division, the atom, cannot be assigned to a particular space. This atom, which cannot be divided, in theory or in reality, cannot exist here or there, and is placeless, as Allah, *al-Bari'*; the creator of forms and shapes, is devoid of space and place. Such an indivisible unit (even if it is part of a greater divisible form), if assigned to a place, would be the opposite of another of the same sort, assigned to a place in contraposition to it. Thus these two units would cancel each other as well as the supposition which resumes this delusion. The indivisible atom is the essence of material things, which cannot be assigned a place. The "soul," the "supreme intelligence," and other names and attributes of that indivisible atom, the essence, cannot be assigned to a body or form or shape, although its existence may be dependent on these material existences for its manifestation.

Allah the Generous One, the Raiser of the dead, the
Guardian of all existence, the Ever-Present.

# THE SECOND FORM OF LIGHT

## *Which Has Three Parts*

### The First Part

**M**an cannot ever forget his essence. That essence is devoid of all illusions and delusions, and is the perfect intelligence. But the animal in man imagines its essence. That is why the essence of the animal is material, it is not spiritual. If one's essence were composite and had parts, although one may forget it sometimes, how could it have been possible for one not to forget it at all times? You forget your body; you are certainly not aware at all times of all the parts of your body, while in your subconscious you are always aware of your essence. That shows that your essence is not a part of your material body. When you say "I," this identity is other and much higher than any part of your material being or the whole of your material being.

## The Second Part
*(Depending on two premises:*
*ever-changing matter,*
*and ever-constant essence)*

Your body continuously flows and dissolves. If the food you eat had not been digested and dissolved, and had not left your body, and if its quantity had been added to your material form, your body would have become immense. Your body is in continuous decomposition. If this continuous birth and death did not occur in your body, and your cells multiplied, your form would have been the size of a giant.

That which is constant, always alive, indivisible, is the opposite of that which changes, divides, dissolves. The essence, the one "I" in your declaration of "I am," is one indivisible, constant and eternal. Therefore, your essence is incorporeal, and cannot be a part of a material being.

As long as your essence is realized within you in a constant state, you are you forever, while with this body you are not. It changes, it is decomposing, it is dying; you don't know it, you don't feel it. How could you be that body? You are much more than that. Allah says in His Holy Book, the Qur'an:

> But Allah doth encompass
> them all from behind.
> (*al-Buruj*, 20)

## The Third Part

The third part consists of three premises:

- One cannot know that which one does not already know.

- The rational is not dependent on measure: when one thinks of the animal kingdom as a common factor, the size of an elephant is of no more importance than the size of a fly.

- The abstract, the nonmaterial, cannot be understood in terms of measure.

As long as you cannot construct the form of something in your mind, you cannot possibly know it, because the realization of a thing has to correspond to something. To understand something is conditional on the existence of its evidence in your mind. Another way to understand a form by comparative thinking is by considering its qualities which are common to other forms. For instance, by considering certain attributes which are common to many animals, you may deduce that an elephant and a fly are equal.

In this kind of thinking, the sizes of these two animals are not compared to each other. Even if that is so among animals, so that a small and a large animal are both animals, what about the essence? In one's existence, it is not commensurate with anything else. Something which cannot be measured cannot be placed within matter that is measurable. Your essence, your rational soul, is not material, nor does it relate to matter. It is free from time and space; therefore it cannot be perceived by the senses. It is a light generated from the *Ahad*, Allah the One and Only, and from the *Samad*, Allah the Eternal and Absolute. [*Ikhlas*, v. 1-2] Man's soul, which is called the cosmic Reason, is an indivisible light which man's conjecturing cannot analyze; it is the sacred light coming from Allah the One and Only, Allah the Eternal and Absolute.

You know enough not to declare that a wall sees or does not see, because to see and not to see are abilities given to that creation which has eyes. Man's rational soul is neither matter nor related to matter. Neither is it a part of this world, nor is it excluded from it. Neither is it dependent upon it, nor is it independent of it. To be dependent or independent are qualities of material things.

The rational soul (the cosmic Reason) is an essence of light which you cannot see. How could a sacred existence such as this — which controls and directs all matter, possesses the knowledge of itself and all that is within its essence, and the knowledge of everything which relates to its essence — be material? This sacred existence, with the influence of spiritual exaltation and rapture, leaves this world of matter and seeks the infinite.

This rational soul has its own powers of realization that help it to see things its way. Some of these powers of observation are evident and some are hidden. The evident ones are the five senses: touching, tasting, smelling, hearing, seeing. The hidden power of observation is a mysterious force like a pool, into which the observations of the five senses flow: a collective consciousness. It is the power that actually experiences dream not coming from the imagination.

Another hidden power is the power of imagination; this is like the source of this collective consciousness. It is the force which preserves the experiences after they have been obtained by the senses. Yet another of these hidden forces is the potential of reason, the power of thought. Analysis by dividing the whole into its parts and collecting the parts into a whole, deriving the universal from the particular, reaching an affirmative conclusion, are all done by this power.

Yet another is the power of conjecture, leading to illusions and delusions, negating the propositions which the mind has confirmed.

It is an evil force which leads man astray from that which the mind proposes: honesty, generosity, justice, valor, munificence. Mind knows that its origin is not of the realm of the senses alone, but belongs to the immaterial world. Mind with the exaltation of reason and spirituality weakens its dependence on the body and wishes to return to the realm of the spirit and of the essence. The power of conjecture, however, considers itself to be of the same material as the mind and at the same level, therefore engaging itself in controversy and dispute. For instance, if the mind claims that beyond the realm of reason there is neither anything nor is there a total vacuum, the power of conjecture says, "No, beyond the world of reason there is either an infinite vacuum, or there is all and everything."

To give an example of the dispute between the power of conjecture and the mind: if one were left alone at night with a corpse, the mind would assure one while delusion would cast fear into one's heart. Illusion plays its tricks especially in affairs which cannot be clearly perceived by the senses. In fact, it denies everything which is not perceivable. It cannot know that the mind and the soul appear unable to perceive things directly only because matter is too coarse, and they are not made of the same material. The faculty of illusion is unaware that it is inherently blind to things immaterial. Matter can know only what is on the surface of water, but not its depth hidden under the surface.

Another hidden power of observation is the power of memory. It preserves all that has happened, and remembers.

All these hidden powers are energies, each having its particular place in the brain. When there is a disruption at that place, the energy belonging to that place is also disturbed, while the other faculties stay safe and secure in their own places. This is how it was proven that each of these faculties is different and that they belong to different places in the brain.

In animals and in the animal in man, there is a double-forked primordial urge. One of its forks is sexual energy, which wishes and attracts that which is pleasant. The other, negativity or anger, repulses that which is unpleasant. The animal also has an energy of struggle (for self-preservation). It is the animal soul both in the animal and in the lower soul in man which contains these energies. It is a vaporous matter composed of bile, sex, blood, and mucus. It is produced in the left cavity of the heart, and receives some energy from the light of the human soul.

The animal soul, the body, and the ego are matter, a part of the created world. The human soul is a part of the Divine, and is under the direct command of Allah. It is only with the enlightenment which the animal soul receives from the human soul that it is able to manifest in the mind.

They ask thee concerning the Soul.
Say: 'The Soul cometh
by the command of my Lord'
(*Bani Isra'il*, 85)

From the highest to the lowest, the realms or centers in man are the Divine Center, the center of the Mind, the center of the Ego, the center of Energies, and the center of Matter.

The proof that (although it is created matter) the animal soul has the fine quality of vapor is that it has to pass through narrow paths in the body. In fact, if there is a blockage in these paths, the part of the body around this path dies. The animal soul serves as a beast of burden for the human soul, providing it with that fine state which can only be obtained through training by the faculty of reasoning received from the enlightenment of the human soul. It becomes disconnected and independent when it dispenses with that faculty of reasoning. This animal soul is in opposition to the Sacred Soul (the highest of souls in man). The description of the Sacred Soul will be given in the section dealing with the souls of the prophets.

The human soul is a sacred light among the sacred lights of Allah, which has no dimension and no place. It rises from Allah and will set in Allah. It is the unraveling of the mystery of the sacred hadith,

*Kuntu khanzan makhfyyian*
*fa khalaqtu al-khalq,*

I was a hidden treasure;
I loved to be known,
so I created creation.

Some among the people, when they realized that the human soul was not material, were deluded into thinking that it must be Allah, and fell into the abyss of blasphemy. Allah is One, Unique. If the souls of Zayd and 'Amr were the same and one soul, then when one realized something, the other would have realized it also. And if one knew, all mankind would have known. However, it is not so. Also, how could this material body and its energies and its powers contain and influence Allah Most High?

Other people thought that the human soul (if not Allah Himself) was a part of Allah, and erred. As Allah is not material, how could He be divisible, and who or what force could tear Him apart?

Some others thought that the human soul was eternal as Allah is Eternal, and that it is independent. If it were so, who is it who separates the soul from its sacred place, brings it into this realm of life, then takes it from this world and brings it to the realm of death and darkness? How can the power of a newborn baby lure it from the world of light and sanctity? How do the souls differ from one another in the eternal realm? They are similar, but do not occupy space or place. They have no action or reaction before taking form in material bodies. Nor do they have attributes which they acquired after their being in the body. So how do they differ? It cannot be that there exists one soul that is divided up among the bodies. For a thing that has no material body cannot be divided. It simply descends into the body if the body is prepared to receive it.

As you know, the flame of a match does not lose anything when setting fire to something combustible. A soul will enter a body, if the body has the potential to receive it, without causing a loss to the Endower of the soul to the body. The One who made the soul is the Creator of All, the All-Compassionate, the One nearer to us than ourselves, the All-Powerful, the Most Holy.

He is Allah besides whom there is no God, the Beneficent, the Merciful, the King Who owns and rules the universe, the Pure devoid of all errors, weaknesses, shortcomings, and heedlessness, the Granter of total security, the Author of Peace.

# THE THIRD FORM OF LIGHT

## *Some Questions for Consideration*

There are three dimensions to the mind in relation to the concept of existence: *wajib*, the necessary; *mumkin*, the possible; and *mumtani'*, the impossible. *Wajib* is an existence whose being is obligatory; *mumkin* is that whose existence or non-existence is not obligatory; *mumtani'* is that which must not exist. *Mumkin*, the possible, added to another possibility, may become either *wajib*, necessary, or *mumtani'*, impossible.

Cause is that through which the existence of something becomes necessary. The possible cannot exist by itself, because if its own existence were sufficient for its being, it would have been not possible, but necessary. Therefore for the possible to exist, there must be a cause. When the cause is fully realized, the effect is produced. For anything to exist, when its existence is dependent on will, time, space, associations, potential, etc., these become its causes for existence. If the cause is not fully realized, the effect cannot be fully realized. If all the reasons and conditions for the existence of a thing are there, and all the reasons and conditions which are unnecessary for the existence of that thing are eliminated, then the existence of that thing is *wajib*, necessary.

When the cause is clear, and some of the evaluations of the possible are positive, the effect becomes clear. At the beginning of the process of conception, the realization of the obvious, which should add up to the cause, may produce an effect which may be different from the cause. Those who accept this proposition explain Allah the Self-Existent by the hadith *kana Allahu wa lam yakun ma'ahu shay'*, "Allah was while nothing else was." Allah is the cause of the Creation, but He is not in need of anything other than Himself. Therefore, He is other than the Creation, yet inseparable from the Creation.

Allah the Ever-Living One, the Owner of all knowledge and power, the Self-Substaining by whom all subsists, the All-Pervasive, the Only One, without partner of likeness.

# THE FOURTH FORM OF LIGHT

## *In Five Sections*

### THE FIRST SECTION

Two things cannot be *wajib*, necessary, at the same time. If the existence of two things is necessary together and at the same time, then their existences would be common and dependent upon each other. It is necessary for them to have a difference to separate one from the other. If one or both depend of necessity on a difference, then their existences are *mumkin*, possible, not necessary or absolute.

It is not possible to conceive two things which do not have a difference between them. When there is no difference between them they are one and the same. There are many kinds of matter in different aspects and conditions, but the *wajib*, the existence of absolute necessity, is only one. The existence of everything else is a possibility necessitating a power which will decide their existence over their nonexistence.

That unequaled power is the Creator, Who is Self-Existent, Whose existence is the One and Only necessary existence, the *wajib*. The One whose existence is the Absolute Necessity cannot be composed of parts. Even if such parts may be conceived, they may only be conceived as a single solution into which everything is dissolved, and these parts in themselves can never be *wajib*, necessary, because there is only One Unique Necessity upon which all depends.

The *sifat*, the descriptive attributes of this Absolute Necessity cannot be a necessity of themselves because the attributes of the Beautiful Names of Allah, the Creator, are the same as His Essence, and inseparable. If the attributes of the One, Unique, Absolute Necessity were themselves necessary existences, they would not have necessitated dependence on a necessity while the Absolute Necessity is not dependent on its attributes. The One and Only Whose existence is the Absolute Necessity does not contain His attributes; neither is it lawful that He invent His attributes. A thing which is self-existent is not under the influence of anything else, neither of itself.

If we were in conscious possession and control of our bodies or a part of our bodies, we would see that what they are doing is other than that which is possible for them to do, while that One and Only Absolute Necessity must be the same at all times and under all conditions as It is ever conscious, free of multiplicity and free of all imperfections.

Man is the microcosm, the universe, the macrocosm. Whatever exists in one exists in the other. The unifying level of all is *al-'aql al-awwal*, the First Cause, the Absolute Necessity, which is the soul of both. It is also the universal intellect, the very first creation of Allah.

Of two existences, the higher is the one whose purpose of existence is for itself. "Allah created the universe for man, and man for Himself," according to a *hadith* (a prophetic tradition). How could he whose perfection is not complete impart perfection to another? Everything which is a composition of multiple elements, in relation to that whose existence is an absolute necessity, enters into the category of the impossible.

Allah the Creator has no equal or opposite, and no relation to any place or dimension. He is totally self-sufficient and complete in His perfection, most noble, and possessor of all light. He is not a manifestation necessitating that which is manifested in Him. He is not an essence to be compared with other essences. All other things, in their lack of resemblance, witness Him, the existence of Absolute Necessity, the First Cause, which made them exist.

Materiality is not a causal condition of all the varieties of existence. The fact that things have their particularities, their forms, their sizes, their manifestations, their movements and their actions which are different from each other, and their different levels which we can compare to the order of the universe, proves that a force other than them is responsible for their creation. If, for instance, their being material were their common causal characteristic, such contrasts and conflicts would not have been in evidence between them.

## THE SECOND SECTION:
### *Determining the Form of Light*

The common point between material things is their being material. Yet every material thing is different from every other in its manifestation of light emanating from it. That light is not proper to material things. It is received from elsewhere and is reflected upon them. The light which is manifested in material things is the only possible shape of light because that light which is not proper to material things is not proper unto itself, but depends upon another. If it were self-dependent, it would have been the Light.

The soul of man is evident within itself because it is of the Light which is self-existent. Yet as we have already shown, the soul descends into the body, there is a force higher than it, and material bodies do not cause its existence. Matter cannot be the cause of the existence of another material thing, because a thing cannot be responsible for the existence of another thing whose existence is higher than it. A single light is necessary to give enlightenment to material things to make their existences higher. That light is the Absolute Necessity, the First Cause, *al-Hayy*, the Ever-living, *al-Qayyum*, the Self-Existent.

The self, the ego in its limited form, witnesses the existence of this Holy Absolute Necessity. It is the Light of all lights, visible to Itself, by Itself, free of all dependence and relation to matter and the visible. It becomes invisible to us and is veiled by the overwhelming power of Its intensity.

## THE THIRD SECTION

It is essential that this overwhelming spiritual power which is One (Unique and Only), in any way which It may manifest itself, has no need of a cause for the existence of Its essence, as other existences do; neither does It need to appear in multiple form. Therefore It bears no resemblance to other existences. When the prerequisite for the existence of a thing is other than what another existence requires, because their requirements do not correspond to each other, they are different from each other. This is the reason and origin of plurality. It is essential for the Absolute Necessity, the First Cause, that It have no aspect of multiplicity. That Absolute Necessity which is essential for the existence of everything else is not material. Therefore It could not have aspects which do not correspond to each other. It is neither a form, a shape, a state, nor a condition that necessitates a place or a space. It is not a soul that needs a body to inhabit. If we suppose an immaterial existence which is a light cognizant of its Creator, Who created it without any model, then a nobler existence than that light is impossible. It is the summit of all that is possible. This essence is possible by itself and in itself, and, through its relation to the One before it, becomes necessary. Receiving the majesty of observation from He Who is before it, it becomes a sacred source itself. But realizing its deficiencies as compared to the majesty of the First Light, it turns into ethereal bodies and forms. So the second sacred essence is to be viewed as being between the Absolute Essence which is above it and the ethereal bodies which are below it.

That is how the incorporeal holy intelligences and heavens and firmaments are formed. Although these immaterial existences are all active forces, they are nothing more than the means through which the First, One, and Unique Holy Source bestows Its munificence. It is the One which makes all move, revolve, and stop. It is the One which is responsible for all. As a strong light does not allow a small light to shine, the Owner of overpowering power, Whose existence is necessary for all existence, the First Cause, the One Unique Sacred Source, will not permit Its means to enlighten the universe independently. The extent of Its enlightenment and the overpowering power of Its perfection are beyond infinity. Its reality prevails over all reality.

## The Last Part of the Third Section, and the Beginning of the Fourth

The universe is divided into three sections. The first is called the realm of the Mind by the ancient philosophers such as Aristotle, Socrates, and Plato.

This realm, called *al-nur al-Muhammadi*, the first created, is also called *'aql al-kull*, the Absolute Mind, which contains the potential of all existence. According to the ancient Greek philosophers, this realm of the Mind is composed of three aspects. The first is its existence, the second is the dependence of its existence on a creative force, and the third is its being a possible existence that contains all other possibilities.

From its aspect of existence, mind is created. From its dependence on a creative force, *nafs*, the self, is created. From its aspect of being a possible existence containing all other possibilities, matter is created. The Prophet (ﷺ) says, *Awwalu ma khalaqa Allahu al-'aql*, "the first creation of Allah is the mind." This is the *'aql al-kull*, the Absolute Mind, the realm of Mind, *logos* of the ancient Greek philosophers.

The mind which is created from its aspect of existence is in two levels. The lower is the *'aql al-ma'ash*, the ordinary intelligence which realizes the affairs of the material world. The higher one is the *'aql al-ma'ad*, the divine intelligence, which realizes spiritual matters, and whose principal function is to lead man to the knowledge of Allah through realizing the mystery of *man 'arafa nafsahu faqad 'arafa rabbahu*, "he who knows himself, knows his Lord."

According to ancient Greek philosophers, all immaterial essence, which cannot be conceived by the senses, and which does not have any association with material existences, is within the realm of the Mind. The second section of the universe is the realm of the *nafs*, the Self (the soul of created beings). The force and perfection of *al-nafs al-tabi'i*, the soul of nature, which holds the created being together and prevents it from disintegrating, and *al-nafs al-nabati*, the soul of vegetation, help the created being to evolve, grow, and multiply. *Al-nafs al-haywani*, the animal soul, helps the created being to move, to sense, and to have a limited will. When these souls are separated from the created being, death occurs.

The realm of the *nafs* includes *al-nafs al-natiqah*, the human soul. *Al-nafs al-natiqah* is of divine origin, as Allah blew with His own breath into Adam (عَلَيْهِ السَّلَام)[4] when He created him from earth, water, fire, and ether. Allah says in a *hadith qudsi*,

*Wa naffastu fihi min ruhi,*

And I breathed My Soul unto him.

*Al-nafs al-natiqah* is that force and perfection which enables man to think, to judge, to witness, and to be.

It evolves in seven stages, from *al-nafs al-ammarah*, the dominating soul mentioned in the Qur'an as:

*Inna al-nafsa la-ammaratun bil-su',*

certainly the nafs, the human soul, impels to evil.
(*Yusuf*, 53)

---

4. عَلَيْهِ السَّلَام or "a.s." is an abbreviation for *'alayhi al-salam*, "peace be upon him," the salutation accompanying mention of the prophets and Messengers.

This is the unregenerate, sinful, human soul that seeks its satisfaction in the lower, earthly desires.

The second is *al-nafs al-lawwamah*, the soul of conscience, mentioned as:

> *Wa la-uqsimu bil-nafs il-lawwamah,*

> I call to witness the self-reproaching soul.
> (*Qiyamah*, 2)

At this stage, the soul is able to judge good and evil; it is conscious of sin sometimes resisting it; it accepts its guilt, repents, and attempts to make amends.

The third stage is *al-nafs al-mulhimah*, the enlightened soul, mentioned as:

> *Wa nafsin wa ma sawwaha fa alhamaha*
> *fujuraha wa taqwaha,*

> By the soul and the proportion and order given to it
> and its enlightenment as to its wrong and its right.
> (*Shams*, 7-8)

At this stage, the soul knows the right and wrong through inspiration, and obeys the voice of its conscience.

The fourth stage is *al-nafs al-mutma'innah*, the soul of bliss and salvation mentioned in the Qur'an as:

> *Ya ayyuha al-nafs al-mutma'innah, irji'ila*
> *rabbiki radiyatan mardiyyah,*

> [To the righteous soul it will be said,]
> 'O thou soul in complete peace and satisfaction,

return to thy Lord well-pleased thyself
and well-pleasing unto Him.'
*(Fajr,* 27-28)

The fifth stage is *al-nafs al-radiyah,* the soul of total
submission, the soul of the real *Muslim,* the one who submits, mentioned as:

*Radiya Allahu 'anhum wa radu 'anhu,*

Allah is well-pleased with them
and them with Allah.
*(Ma'idah,* 122)

This is the soul which accepts and is satisfied with Allah's
will, and submits to it.

The sixth stage is *al-nafs al-mardiyyah,* the soul
which is close to its Creator, and with which Allah is well-
pleased, as mentioned in Surah *Fajr,* v. 27-28, Surah
*Ma'idah,* v. 122, and Surah *Bayinnah,* v. 8. This is a stage
where the soul receives the good pleasure of Allah and the
good pleasure is mutual. The soul has become completely
identified with Allah's universal will; losing its own will,
the soul is in the state of *fana fillah,* lost in Allah.

The final state of *al-nafs al-natiqah,* the human soul,
is *al-nafs al-zakiyyah* or *al-nafs al-kamilah,* the purified,
the perfect soul mentioned in the Qur'an as:

*Qad aflaha man zakkaha,*

Truly he succeeds
who purifies it.
*(Shams,* 9)

This is the soul of *al-insan al-kamil*, the perfect man, as man is meant to be, the microcosm of the whole universe, who contains all that is in the universe.

The world of *nafs*, the self, and the world of *al-nafs al-natiqah*, the human soul, have no form or dimension of their own, yet they inhabit material forms, and exist within the world of matter. *Al-nafs al-natiqa*, the human (or rational) soul, exists within spiritual beings and the firmament and in mankind, and is of two kinds. The one which inhabits bodies is also of two kinds, the ethereal and the elemental. The higher and stronger light is *al-ruh al-kuddus*, the Holy Spirit, that the philosophers call *al-'aql al-fa'al*, the Active Mind, which like a compassionate father guides the human mystery, sustains the human spirit and leads us to perfect wisdom.

All these are holy lights, but the first created existence is *al-'aql al-awwal*, the First and Universal Mind, *al-nur al-Muhammadi*, the Light of Muhammad through which shone the rays of the First Light. As the rays of the First Light increased reflecting from heart to heart without words or letters, the Mind increased, and through the revelation of this enlightenment, became manifold.

Because we apply the rules of causality, this light revealed to us reflecting from heart to heart seems very close to us. In reality, because of its overwhelming intensity, what is farthest seems nearest to us. The nearest is the Light of the Light. Don't you see that of two spots, one black and the other white, lying on the same plane, the white seems closer to us? The white is most becoming to things which are visible. The First Light is the highest of the high and the nearest of the near.

All praise to the Holy Essence, the Source, the Cause

of All, free of all defect, perfect, highest above all; farther than the farthest, yet nearer than the nearest because of the penetration of the overwhelming power of Its Light.

## THE FIFTH SECTION

Allah *al-Bari'*, the Maker who invented and brought into being from nonexistence to existence all else except Himself, is eternal. As He, the Maker of all else, is eternal, those whose existences are possible and depend for their being on Him will also exist forever. Everything whose existence is possible depends only on Allah for its existence, because Allah *al-Bari'*, the Maker, existed before everything else.

His preexistence is not dependent on time or conditions as is our existence: for instance, we may put something off until Thursday or until Zayd comes. It is incontestable that nothing existed before Him. The Creator, the Maker, is absolutely unchangeable. All creation is His Will. He will not create that which He did not want, nor will He want that which He has not wanted.

You know that light comes from the sun, and you know that the sun is not made out of light. How then could you doubt that Allah the Creator, the Maker of all, is just and free from all defect in His Creation? Light keeps shining, and one light reflects upon another. Does the sun become any less? Do its rays diminish?

Allah the Just, the One Who knows the inner essence of things and the hidden. The One Who is beneficent to His creation in the finest of ways. Allah the Clement.

# THE FIFTH FORM OF LIGHT

A cause is needed to constitute a new existence as new, and the consideration of causality seems to be a continuum where there is no end nor beginning to the occurrence of new causes producing the appearances of new existences. This proves that as long as one existence is qualified and dependent upon yet another causal existence, it cannot be the first of new existences.

That which necessitates renewal in itself is movement. Of all movements, the absolute uninterrupted continuous one is a circular movement. Circular and perpetual movements can only be produced by the revolving of the firmament. This is the cause of the occurrence of all the happenings of this material world. Allah, the Creator, the Maker Who transfers existences from nonexistence to existence is unchanging; and in His immutableness, He cannot be the cause of these new movements. If it were not for the revolving movements of the firmament, no new existence would have had an originating causal existence. The revolving spheres of heaven, the movements of the firmament, are not natural movements, because these movements deviate from a point intended. A thing which moves according to its nature stops at the point which its nature intends to reach, because it cannot escape that point which is desirable by its nature. Therefore we deduce that this movement is a movement initiated by will.

# The First Part

What gives life and motion to the revolving of the firmament is its Essence. For that which sets into motion the form of the firmament is a volitional thrust. The beginning of the movement of its form is this thrust of the firmament, which is an involuntary movement.

If we consider the form of the firmament and its essence to be independent of each other, then the motion of the form, set off by the thrust of the essence becomes involuntary. However, if we consider the essence and the form to be one, then the movement of the firmament is a willful act. In this respect the firmament is alive and conscious, but does not need nourishment, nor to be born, nor to grow. It has no desires, no opposition, no resistance. It has neither anger nor negativity. As it gives no value to lowly things, there is no lowliness in its movement.

There are two kinds of possible existences: the abstract incorporeal ones and those which have material forms. Both the abstract and the material, like the incorporeal intelligence and the material firmament, exist in the best possible existence for them. They cannot be any more perfect. Man who is the microcosm of the whole of the created universe, has the potential of total perfection, although his natural state falls short of that.

When we cleanse ourselves from the relationships and concerns of our flesh and submerge ourselves in the reflection of the magnificence and might of our Creator, the Maker Who transfers existences from nonexistence to existence and the illuminating light which generates from Him, we find our essence beautified and shining with the enlightening of the divine illumination and manifestation of Allah, and we reach our desired goal. How can we doubt the states of the divinely endowed personalities who are safe, being distant from this world of contradictions and its malice, while we have no doubt that we will reach the greatest felicity by saving ourselves from the slavery of the flesh? These blessed beings, in their divinely guided states, have no preoccupations nor worries to interrupt the continuous illumination which they receive. If their movement toward their desired goal were not exempt from interruption, their advancement would have been impaired.

The beloved of Allah in these higher states do not resemble each other. They are lights, and they are the causes and the saviors. They observe the sacred realms through the intermediaries between themselves and the Divine Creator. From the enlightenment received through seeing the divine, potentials appear in them. With the regeneration of movement, illumination is renewed, and this continues. Through this continuous succession the new incidents in this lower world follow one upon the other. If this illumination and motion did not exist, there would have appeared only a limited amount of Allah's generosity and munificence, and at a point the divine illumination would have ceased.

Allah's munificence and generosity continues through various levels and varieties in the continuum of this material universe. The total motion originates from incidents occurring in this world of disorder and sedition. If it were not for the total motion and what it carries, this lowly world and the endless renewal of things would have no meaning. We must not imagine any other influence upon this general harmony except that of Allah. The movement of the firmament is not a cause for the existence of things, yet it does form potentials. The formation of these potentials is the appearance of new possibilities in things which dispose them to receiving new illuminations.

Allah, the Maker, is free of all changes. There is no change in His Holy Essence which might lead to changes which distinguish His manifestations. The continuity of Allah's munificence, and the continuous existence of the divine lovers and the renewal of events and their movements secure the benefits for the created beings in the lower worlds. The motion of the firmament is not responsible for the invention of things, but it forms capacities in them. Allah, the Maker, gives to everything according to the degree of its capacity. As long as the act is unchanged, the effect and the affected are not renewed. Change is possible only by a change in the disposition of the possible. Renewal is possible only by the renewed possibility in the affected element.

It is lawful that the effect of a Unique being be renewed. This does not happen by change in His state, but may happen by the possible change of the state of the mirror which reflects Him. For instance, if a human being were a totally unchanging, immobile entity surrounded by many large and small, clear and dim mirrors, the varied colors and forms appearing in these mirrors will not be due to changes in the attributes of this entity but due to the different characteristics of the mirrors. This is how Allah Most High, the Maker, ties the unchanging constant to the constant and continuously renews the new, so that He can continue to pour upon us His good and His illumination and His munificence.

The generosity and the munificence of our Maker cannot be lacking or intermittent. Generosity is doing that which has to be done without expecting any return. The Absolutely Rich One is Allah, for He expects no rewards and has no needs. He is the Light of Lights Who needs no other than Himself for His perfection and essence. In all His doings there is never hostility or prejudice. The essence of His Holy Being is the munificence of His mercy and beneficence. His immense kingdom and the essence of everything in it is for Him. His Essence is not for anything or anybody. One cannot conceive this universe of existences to be more perfect than it is, because His Holy Essence cannot contain anything petty or insignificant. But in an endless and inexhaustible manner He requires the better, and better than the better. As the light is brighter than the reflection of its reflection, it is an impossibility for the universe of existences to be more complete than it is. It cannot be. Something inconceivable is not within the power of the powerful. Those who conjecture on the basis of both good and bad coming from Allah are those who imagine that the high is favored over the low, that there is not another universe belonging to Allah behind this darkness, and that there is not any other creation except this creation. They do not know that if this universe of existences were other than it is, it is then that badness and harm would be made necessary and the total order would be destroyed from one end to the other. The state in which we are is the highest level that is possible for us. ("In the creation of possibilities, the existent is the most wonderful, the most novel," according to al-Ghazali. "When it was asked, 'What is the intention of Allah in creating creation?,' it was answered, 'Allah's intention is realized in the existing state of the creation,' " as we are told by Hadrat Ja'far al-Sadiq.)

The last stage is another realm than this where our souls are cleansed of our flesh and our egos will return. The inhabitants of that exalted realm do not participate in affairs such as putting people who have hidden their sins to shame by exposing them, grabbing orphans from the arms of their wet nurses, punishing the innocent, spreading ignorance, misleading people, exalting the worthless, abasing the worthy, and injuring the men of knowledge. Their occupation is watching the lights of Allah's manifestation in every aspect of life. If the seeming disorder in certain parts of the universe were useful, it would only be useful in causing disorder in other parts of the universe where disorder is necessary. While the behavior of higher realms is not for the sake of lower realms, those who belong to the former under the force and majesty of the divine stations which envelop them and the rays of the divine nature and the lights of the self-existing Allah, are not concerned with anything else; they do not even have the strength to be concerned with themselves. They are pure light, therefore they know the hidden as well as the evident. Nothing can be hidden from their knowledge.

The fact that the firmaments are not composed of parts and that their order cannot be disturbed and that they are in continuous motion is a proof that they are nonelemental. And the ineffectiveness of the lightness of the heat which can only rise, and the heaviness of the cold which can only descend, and the wetness which in its composition easily accepts separation and connection, and the dryness which resists separation and connection show that there is no division nor unification in the firmaments. The movements of these firmaments are not vertical; they do not move towards the center, nor do they move away from the center. Perhaps their movements are that which are in between the two, that is to say, circular. These firmaments are neither heavy nor light, neither hot nor cold, neither wet nor dry. They have a fifth nature. If the heavens had not englobed the earth, once the sun set in the west, it would not return to the east. Or this would have been possible if there were double, twin days. Hence all the firmaments are global. In fact, they have their own reasoning and are related to the divine lights through their love for them, and are totally submitted to that Source Who rendered them self-renewing. They are not lifeless in the realm of ether.

## The End of the Fifth Form of Light

In the realm of existences the first relationship is the relationship between the Essence, which is present and existent, and the One Who is Self-Existent. This relationship is the mother and the highest form of all relationships and is attached with love to the Self-Existent One. Unable to surround with the depth of its own inner light, it is overwhelmed with the self-existence of the Self-Existent. This relationship has two aspects: love and might. One of these aspects is the higher and more noble. The attributes of this relationship have penetrated every realm, so that every part has a counterpart. Thus the essences are divided into matter and non-matter, and nonmatter overwhelms matter and is the beloved and cause of all matter; one of these counterparts is baser. In addition, the essence that differentiates matter is divided into two counterparts. Of these counterparts one is high and overwhelming, and the other is at a lower level and passive. Matter itself is divided into counterparts, the ethereal and the elemental. Some ethereal matters are divided into two counterparts: felicity and overwhelming power, or the sun and the moon, which are like the mind and the ego. The sublime and the base, the right and the left, the East and the West, the male and the female in animals are all examples of these. In the evolution of the first relationship, the perfect and the lacking are joined by marriage. This is what is understood in the verse of the Holy Qur'an,

> And of everything We have created pairs, that
> you may receive instruction.
> (*Zariyat*, 49)

The sun is the highest and the most honored of existences, the most luminous, the most honored and brilliant of all matter, the illuminator and the sustainer of the universe, the one which overwhelms darkness and brings daylight, the chief of the heavens, the beneficent donor of light to heavenly bodies which expects no return. The sun is one of the greatest and most distinguished manifestations of the glory and the essence of Allah. How great is the glory and majesty of the One Who started and rendered self-renewing all this!

Blessed be Allah, the Most Beautiful of all creators.

The One Who plans and rules the universe and all that happens therein. The generous Pardoner of repentant sinners, the Benefactor without conditions.

# THE SIXTH FORM OF LIGHT

The soul (the Cosmic Reason) is not disrupted by the disruption of the body, because the soul is not the kind of light which requires space and place. It possesses neither opposite nor opposition. Its generator is eternal, and it is continuous with its source. Its relation with the material body depends upon the yearning or the indifference they have toward each other.

As you know, the pleasure and the pain of every state is in accordance with its own particular characteristics and with its degree of perfection. The fragrance depends upon the relationship between the thing smelled and the one who smells; taste depends upon the relation between that which is tasted and the one who tastes; and knowledge depends upon the relation of the thing to be learned and the one who wishes to learn. It depends upon whether one is worthy of the other. The perfection of the substance of the enlightened intelligence is colored by the knowledge of the universal order and truth. In summary, while the acquisition of the knowledge of the beginning and the end depends upon one's purification from material forces and from one's flesh, and the absence of this perfection creates the opposite condition, the experiences of pleasure and pain are also dependent on these conditions.

Pleasure and pain can exist even if they are not experienced. It is as if the unconscious inquirer says: If the happiness of man depends upon his ability to conceive, how is it that we do not feel any pleasure or joy while we are learning? The answer to that question is that joy and pleasure depend upon the existence of certain conditions between the conceived and the conceiver. For instance, the property of burning of fire is dependent upon its coming into contact with something flammable. In the absence of the quality of flammability, fire does not contain the property of burning. Someone in shock or lost in excessive drunkenness would not feel pain if he were being beaten nor could he feel pleasure if he were in the arms of his beloved. As long as the soul is preoccupied with the flesh, neither will it suffer from villainies nor will it be pleased with virtues because it is in a state of heavy drunkenness with the intoxicant of nature. It has lost itself with the violence of this drunkenness.

When the soul leaves the body, that of the unfortunate rebel against Allah is tortured by the deep ignorance into which it has sunk, by the state of dark wretchedness, and by the desire and longing which it still feels for the world of the senses.

*Wa qad hila baynahum wa baynama yashtahuna.*

The hell-bound and that which they
desire are separated.
(*Saba'*, 54)

In the state of these rebels the secret of this verse is manifested. Neither their eyes see nor their ears hear. Neither the flicker of this world of the senses nor the illumination of the sacred Light reaches them. They are bewildered in the darkness. Cut off from both lights, they are submerged in misery and despair and terrible fears. They are like the ones who are afflicted with the worst condition of melancholy, continuously tortured by grief and anxiety. While that is the condition of melancholics, imagine furthermore the state of those yearning only for material pleasures, having lost all other hope and having fallen into the bottomless pit of hellish darkness. Meanwhile the purified souls of those who in all their aspects have opted for the good and the virtuous have reached eternal bliss, having attained bounties unseen, unheard of, unimaginable, close to their Creator, submerged in the Intellect. The purified souls return to their Creator Who is victorious over human bodies which harbor dark forces, Who destroys the images of darkness, and Who has created man in the best and most noble form. They become Allah's neighbors. They are crowned with the crowns of closeness in the realm of spirits, near to the Lord of the Universe, the Holy Spirit. Those souls are eternally attracted to their Creator in the same manner that a metal needle is attracted to a magnet. Just as there is no comparison between the senses and the soul (for the awareness of the soul is more perfect and comprehensive than that of the senses), there is no comparison between the lights of Allah and the rational soul, and the senses. The taste of the higher mind is in love with its essence and its essence is the beloved of that and everything else.

There is no resemblance nor relation between the evolved state of the virtuous souls, who have left the darkness of forms and who have been honored by the luminosity of Allah in the higher realms of the universe of spirits, and the taking shape of common material things under the rays of the sun. Those who deny spiritual tastes are those who are drowned with their animal lusts. They prefer the animal in them over holy human beings and angels.

He is the Creator, the Giver of shape and character, the Bestower of most beneficent gifts, the Pardoner of sins, the Overwhelming One.

# THE SEVENTH FORM OF LIGHT

## *On Prophethood*

The human soul, which is also called the Cosmic Reason, is one of the essences of the universe of spirits. This spiritual realm is the universe of abstractions and conceptions. When this essence is freed from the preoccupations of the material powers of the body, eating, and sleeping decrease, awareness increases, the flesh awakens, and the spiritual essence is strengthened by receiving divine virtues. These spiritual virtues are of four kinds. The first is wisdom, which is the justification for the blessing of the intellectual powers which one is given. The second is valor, the justification of the powers of wrath and strength. The third is chastity, the justification of the sexual and sensual powers. The fourth is true justice, the justification of all the powers which one is given. This true justice is a very fine line between excess and insufficiency. The slightest deviation becomes injustice. This true justice is the way of the prophets.

Every once in a while the soul finds its way toward the sacred realm, learning that which it knew not from its Holy Sustainer to which it belongs. The soul also reaches the souls of the celestial spheres which are aware of their own movements and the causes necessitating their movements. Like a mirror that is decorated by the image placed in front of it, the soul begins to understand a number of secrets, both in a waking and a sleeping state. Sometimes it almost sees strange images from its destined portion of the mysteries of the spiritual realm which are reflected upon its powers of imagination. These same images which pass through one's mind may also appear in the world of the senses. Words once spoken are heard, or invisible, and unknown things become visible, sometimes clear, sometimes obscure according to one's connection and the intensity of one's wish. The obscurity which causes these strange occurrences in people who are lost to their material selves cannot have any variation in clarity or obscurity, because these variations belong to the observation of material things under light. These visions are within a darkness which is a material shadow. This also applies to the play of the devil in false dreams, and even to the imaginary stories of sincere dreams.

Sometimes the sacred soul through its contact with the divine reaches to a state of excitement, joy, and felicity and comes face to face with Allah's illumination. If you have seen a piece of iron heated by fire that becomes red hot like the fire and does what fire does, then do not doubt that when the essence of the soul submits itself with obedience, it can transmit the effects of divine illumination. The whole universe submits and obeys the divine when it attains divine enlightenment and is enlightened by the holy light.

There are such great men who have been blessed with the brilliant enlightenment of truth. They have turned their faces to the divine, opened their hands in supplication, wishing and expecting the manifestation of the very essence of Allah in addition to the manifestation of Allah's attributes and actions which they have already received. The one who received the eternal guidance of Allah and wished to reach his Creator as a part of his heavenly sustenance and his lot, opening his eyes, found Allah's divine beauty and divine light hidden under the overwhelming magnificence and power of a divine light which no mind has conceived nor will ever conceive. He saw a large crowd praying for Allah's mercy, visible with the light emanation from the secret Greatest Name of Allah written on the arch of Allah's dominion.

To believe in the truth of the prophets and to have faith in them is a sacred requirement for those who have an inner eye. These select persons have shown the distinction of truth from falsehood by the examples which they transmitted, as is contained in the Holy Qur'an:

And such are the examples set forth for mankind, but
only those understand them who have knowledge.
*(Ankabut, 43)*

and as another prophet said, "I wish to begin talking by the use of examples and parables."[5]

The interpretation of the inner meaning of all the verses of all the holy books which were revealed and descended to all the prophets belongs to *Farkilit*, who is honored by the greatest portion of divine light.[6]

---

5. These lines point to a conviction of Hz. Suhrawardi that the prophets, through the examples of certain parables, revealed certain mysteries and truths which may be understood by "those who have knowledge," yet are meant to be divulged openly only on the last day of the worlds, the Day of Last Judgment. This doctrine was used as part of the evidence by which the ultra-orthodox jurists of his time condemned him to death.

6 In the original Aramaic version of the Bible, this word appears as *Parkilit*, which becomes *Farkilit* in Arabic, which does not contain the letter P. In the Greek translation of the Bible, it appears as

The Prophet Jesus (﷽) said, "Truly the One who created me and sustained me will send the *Farkilit* in my name. He will teach you all things." [John 14:26] [7]

In the Holy Qur'an it is said,

*thumma in na alaina-bayanah,*

Again on Us rests the explaining of it.
(*Qiyamat*, 19)

In Arabic the particle *thumma*, "again," is used to indicate delay, meaning postponing and performing at a later time. The word *bayan*, "explanation," means clarification through the use of examples.

―――――――――

*Paraclete*, which means, in Greek, "Comforter." Jesus Christ says, "I am the apostle of God sent to you, confirming the law that came before me, and giving glad tidings of an apostle to come after me whose name shall be Ahmad." [*Saff*, v. 6] We are here told that Jesus (﷽) gave news of Ahmad, a title of the Prophet (ﷺ), meaning "Most Praised." This is the meaning of an alternative Greek transcription of the Aramaic, *Periclytos*.

The *Paraclete* is called in the Bible "the spirit of Truth" [John 14:17]. The Qur'an also calls the Prophet "The Truth." [*Bani Isra'il*, v. 81] Among the marks of the spirit of Truth in the Gospel are that he would abide forever [John 14:16], would teach all things, and would speak what he hears from God [John 14:26, 16:13]. The prophet who "shall speak unto them all that I shall command him," was also foretold to Moses in Deuteronomy 18:18-19, where news is given of one "like unto thee." It is thought that the *Jalal*, or majesty, of the Truth was manifested in Moses, and its *Jamal*, or beauty, in Jesus, while both elements were combined in the person of the Holy Prophet (ﷺ).

7. Hz. Suhrawardi interprets and translates the Prophet Jesus' use of the expression "Our Father" as his and others' Creator and Sustainer, very much in the sense of the word *Rabb*, "Lord," or *Rabb ul-alamin*, "Lord of the Universes," Who creates and sustains all His creation. Thus the prophet Jesus (﷽.) addresses Allah as the Creator and Sustainer of himself and other servants of Allah.

There is no doubt that the light from the realm of spirits pours upon and saves those who wish and yearn for it and that divine light spreads to open the path of truth. So it is with the sudden light of quick lightning which abstracts the sensible, and so it was with the news which was brought from the swift Night Journey into the invisible world.[8]

O Lord Who is our Sustainer, we believe in You and we have faith in the truth of the prophets which You have sent to us. We know that the holy among Your servants and the spiritual levels reach to the light by light, yet even fools who sometimes wish to reach the light, leaving the light for the darkness and following the dark path to the light become a lesson for the wise and give light to their understanding, and become the cause for their high rank and closeness to Allah. Those spiritual winds which You send for them lead them to the highest stations where all they do is glorify the light on Your Face, carry the holy books, hold onto the wings of the angels, embrace the rays

---

8. Hz. Suhrawardi refers to the night of Ascension as "the swift night." On his Ascension, when the Prophet (ﷺ) left his bed in the house of Umm Hani, he brushed against a leaf. In his journey he observed Mecca, Jerusalem, and many heavenly realms up to the very Throne of Allah, and all the divine signs therein. As he returned to his bed in the house of Umm Hani, that leaf was still trembling from his slight touch upon his departure, and his bed was still warm. In Sufi terminology this is called "time expansion," when a split second is enlarged and spreads to include affairs which ordinarily necessitate many years to be actualized.

In the Holy Qur'an it is said, "*And He it is Who sends the winds as heralds of glad tidings going before His mercy; and We sent down pure water from the sky*" [*Furqan*, v. 48]. For the one who lights the lightning upward, it is made known that the divine path is open. The open path is the path of many a perfect man who pass through its stations.

of the lights, drawing them upwards, and hope to attain intimacy with Allah with the help of these marvelous and solitary states. These are the ones who withdraw to the heavens yet appear in this world. O Divine One, awaken the souls buried in tombs of unconsciousness so that they remember and glorify You. Give us the full share of our lot of knowledge and patience as these are the source of all virtue. Give us the gift of being pleased with that which is destined for us. Let the illumination by the pure light of the soul be our path and let the selfless brotherhood of faith be our companion. You are the one who gives only good to all the universes through Your generosity and munificence. Allah is the best of all helpers.

Allah's salutations, pleasure, peace, and blessings be upon His Holy Prophet.

Allah the Sustainer, the All-Knowing, the One Whose orders and manifestations are wisdom, the Loving One and the only One worthy of love, the Powerful, Glorious, and Generous.

# IN THE NAME OF
# ALLAH THE MERCIFUL
# AND THE COMPASSIONATE

All praise and grace is due to Allah the Most Generous, the Most Wise, the Ultimate Guide, the Giver of Faith and Hope. All peace and blessings and benedictions be upon His beloved, the unlettered Prophet (ﷺ) whom He has cleansed of all false knowledge in order to teach him the pure truth, and upon his progeny and companions and helpers, and upon the ones whom he loved and the ones who loved him, and upon the ones whom he loves and who love, obey, and follow him.

The spiritual teachers, the *murshid*s, who are the true fathers, are bound to give to their true sons and daughters, the *murid*s, the greatest gift possible to give in this world, and that is sincere advice.

The first portion of that gift, that spiritual nourishment, is the knowledge of Allah's orders to His creation, the *'ilm al-shari'ah*. This knowledge is a reason for one's being. It is an obligation upon all, it is the force of life, the light of intelligence, without which one is dead.

The second portion is the knowledge of the path to truth, the *tariqah*. It is not a path traced on a map, but a road upon which to walk. It is a necessity, for the sign of life is movement, from birth to death, from this life to the Hereafter, from worse to better, from less to more, from many to one, from falsehoods to truth, from anxiety to peace. It is a response to the divine invitation *irji'*, "*Come!*" — "Come here, come to Me."

The third portion of that gift is *ma'rifah*, which is a means to wisdom, the space that contains the divine secrets that one must discover.

The fourth and the last portion of the gift that the spiritual father bestows upon his spiritual children is the *haqiqah*, which is in reality a gift of Allah, the Ultimate Truth, that comes through the hands of the spiritual teacher.

Knowledge is like water, the source of life. Look around you, it is everywhere: torrents of rain, rivers, lakes, oceans. . . . Yet all receive in accordance with their destiny, in accordance with their need, in the amount of the size of their cup.

Allah, the One Whose existence is endless.

# EPILOGUE

As I was wandering in this temporal world, Allah led me to a straight path. Walking on it in a state between sleep and awakening, as if in a dream, I reached a city which was enveloped in darkness. It was so vast, I could neither see nor conceive of its limits. This city contained everything which was created. There were people from all nations and races. So crowded were the streets that one could hardly walk, so noisy was it that one could hardly hear oneself or others. All the ugly actions of all the creatures, all the sins known and unknown to me, surrounded me. In awe and amazement I watched the strange scene.

Far in the distance, in the apparent center of this city, there was yet another city, with high walls, huge in size.

What I observed all around me led me to think that never, since the beginning of time, had a ray of light from the sun of truth fallen upon this city. Not only were the sky and the roads and houses of this city in total darkness, but its citizens, who were like bats, had minds and hearts as dark as night. Their nature and their behavior were like those of wild dogs. Growling and fighting with each other for a mouthful of food, obsessed by lust and anger, they killed and tore each other apart. Their only pleasure was in drinking and in shameless sex, without discrimination of male and female, wives and husbands or others. Lying, cheating, gossiping, slander, stealing was their custom, with total absence of concern for others, conscience, or fear of Allah. Many among them called themselves *Muslim*s. In fact, some were considered by them to be wise men — shaykhs, teachers, men of knowledge, and preachers.

Some among them who became aware of Allah's commandments, of that which is right and lawful in the eyes of Allah and men, and of that which Allah forbids, tried to act upon these and found satisfaction in it and could no longer associate with the people of the city. Neither could the people of the city tolerate them. I heard they took refuge in the walled city I had seen in the center of this realm.

I stayed in this outer city for a while. At length I found someone who could hear me and understand what I said. I asked him the name of the place. He told me that it was *Ammara*, the imperious city, the city of freedom, where everyone did what he pleased. I inquired about their state. He said that it was the city of joy, which derived from carelessness and heedlessness. In the beautiful darkness that surrounded it, each one thought that he was the only one. I asked him the name of their ruler. He informed me that he was called '*Aql al-Ma'ash*, His Highness Cleverness, and that he was an astrologer, a sorcerer, an engineer who engineered things, a doctor who gave life to the ones who otherwise would die, an intelligent learned king who had no equal in this world. His advisers and ministers were called Logic, his judges depended on the ancient Law of Common Sense, his stewards were called Imagination and Daydreaming. He said that all the citizens were totally loyal to their ruler, not only respecting and appreciating him and his government, but loving him, for they all felt an affinity to him in their nature, in their customs, in their behavior.

I, possessing the same intelligence, and with it knowing that indeed the king of this city was the perfect master of all the sciences of this world, wished to learn these sciences in order to be rich and famous. I stayed for a while in the king's service and learned from him many clever things. I learned commerce, politics, military sciences, manufacturing arms, the law of man, and arts to glorify man. I became world-renowned. As men pointed me out with their fingers and talked about me, my ego rejoiced. Since all the parts of my being were totally under the influence of my worldly intelligence, they all found energy in the rejoicing of my ego and rushed to spend that energy in worldly delights and the pleasures of the flesh, without any consideration of whether all this hurt others, or even myself.

Something inside of me at times saw that all this was wrong, but I had no strength nor ability to prevent it. That part of me which saw was pained, and wished to get out of the darkness of this city. One such day, when the pain was most acute, I went to my master the king, His Highness Cleverness, and daringly asked, "How is it that the men of knowledge of your realm never act upon their knowledge and fear Allah? How is it that none in this city fear the punishment of Allah, while they fear your punishment? How is it that there is no light here, nor outside, nor in your people's hearts? How is it that your subjects appear as human beings, yet their nature is like that of wild animals, and worse still?"

He answered, "I — the one who can figure out how to derive personal benefit from this world, even if my benefit is their loss — am their ideal. I have an agent in each of them. They are my servants and the servants of my agents in them, but I also have a master who guides me, and that is the Devil. No one here is able to change his way, and all are content and think of themselves as better than others. None will to change, and therefore they will not change."

When I heard that, I wished to leave that city, and intended to escape. But knowing the king's strength and control over everything, I asked his permission to leave. "O my absolute ruler," I said, "You have done so much for this humble servant of yours and have given me all I have. What a joyful life I have led under your rule! You clothed me with rich furs, gave me companions for fun and games. Neither drunkenness nor gambling have you forbidden. I have tasted all the pleasures, and I feel I have had my share. Did you know that I came to this city as a traveler? Permit me now to go to that big castle that I see in the middle of your city."

The king answered me, saying, "I rule over that castle also. That district is called *Lawwama*, Self-Reproach, but its people are not the same as we are here. In this imperious city of ours, our idol is the Devil. Neither he nor I blame anyone for what they do. Therefore, none regret what they have done, for we live in imagination. In the City of Self-Reproach, imagination does not have total power. They also do what is called sin — they commit adultery, they satisfy their lust with men and women alike, they drink and gamble, steal and murder, gossip and slander as we do — but often they see what they have done, and regret and repent."

As soon as I finished talking with my master, Cleverness, I rushed to the gates of the City of Self-Reproach. Over the gates was written *at-ta'ibu min adh-dhanbi ka-man la adhnaba*, "The one who has repented is like the one who has never committed a sin."

I gave the password by repenting for my sins, and entered the city.

I saw that this city was considerably less crowded than the City of Darkness from which I had come. I would say that its population was half that of the city I had left.

After I had stayed there for awhile, I found out that there was a man of knowledge who knew the Holy Qur'an and expounded upon it. I went to him and saluted him. He returned my salutation and wished Allah's peace and blessings upon me. Although I had been told by the ruler of the City of Darkness that he ruled here also, I checked with my teacher, asking him the name of their ruler. He confirmed that they were under the jurisdiction of His Highness Cleverness, but that they had their own administrators, whose names were Arrogance, Hypocrisy, Bigotry, and Fanaticism.

Among the population were many men of knowledge, many men who appeared to be virtuous, devout, pious, and righteous. I made friends with these men and found them to be afflicted with arrogance, egotism, envy, ambition, bigotry, and, in their friendship, insincerity. They were hostile to each other setting traps for each other. What I can say for the best of them is that they prayed and tried to follow Allah's commandments because they feared Allah's punishment and Hell, and hoped for an eternal, pleasurable life in Paradise.

I asked one of them about the City of Darkness outside the walls, and complained about the people there. He agreed with my complaints, and said that the population of that city consisted of corrupt, seditious, murderous nonbelievers. They had no faith, nor did they ever pray. He said they were drunkards, adulterers, pederasts; they were totally unconscious and heedless. But from time to time, by some mysterious guidance, they were led to the City of Self-Reproach. Then they realized what they had done and regretted, repented, and asked for forgiveness. In their city, he said, they did not know what they were doing, so it never occurred to them to regret or to ask forgiveness. Therefore they did not help each other, and no one interceded for them.

When I had first come to the City of Self-Reproach, I had seen that in its center there was yet another castle. I asked the learned inhabitant about it. He said that it was called *Mulhima*, the City of Love and Inspiration. I asked about its ruler, and was told that he was called '*Aql al-Ma'ad*, His Highness Wisdom, Knower of Allah. This king, said my informant, had a prime minister whose name was Love.

"If ever any one of us enters the City of Love and Inspiration," he went on, "we don't accept him back to our city. For anyone who goes there becomes like all the rest of that city's population — totally attached to that prime minister. He falls in love with him, and is ready to give up anything — all that he has, his possessions, his family and children, even his life — for the sake of that prime minister called Love. Our sultan, His Highness Cleverness, finds this attribute absolutely unacceptable. He fears the influence of those who have this quality, for both their loyalty and their actions seem to be illogical and are not understandable by common sense.

"We hear that the people of that city call upon Allah chanting and singing, even with the accompaniment of the reed flute and tambourines and drums, and that doing so they lose their senses and go into ecstasy. Our religious leaders and theologians find this unacceptable according to our orthodox rules. Therefore, none of them even dreams of setting foot in the City of Love and Inspiration."

When I heard that, I felt a terrible distaste for the City of Self-Reproach, and ran to the gates of the blessed City of Love and Inspiration. I read over the door *bab ul-jannati maktub: la ilaha illa Llah.* I recited aloud the sacred phrase *la ilaha illa Llah* — "There is no god but Allah" — prostrated myself, and offered my sincere thankfulness. At this, the gates opened and I entered.

Soon I found a dervish lodge, where I saw the high and the lowly, the rich and the poor together, as if one single being. I saw them loving and respecting each other, serving each other with regard, reverence, and deference, in a continuous state of pure joy. They were talking, singing — their songs and their talk captivating, beautiful, always about Allah and the Hereafter, spiritual; removed from all anxiety and pain, as if living in Paradise. I did not hear or see anything that resembled dispute or quarrel, anything harmful or damaging. There was no intrigue or malice, envy or gossip. I felt immediately a peace, comfort, and joy among them.

I saw a beautiful old man, consciousness and wisdom shining through him. I was attracted to him and went over and addressed him: "O my dearest, I am a poor traveler and a sick one at that, seeking a remedy for my sickness of darkness and unconsciousness. Is there a doctor in this City of Love and Inspiration to cure me?"

He stayed silent for awhile. I asked his name. He told me his name was *Hidaya,* Guidance. Then he said, "My nickname is Truthfulness. Since time immemorial not a single untruth has passed from these lips. My duty and my charge are to show the way to the ones who sincerely seek union with the Beloved. And to you I say,

> And serve thy Lord until there comes to
> thee that which is certain.
> (*Hijr*, 99)

And remember the name of thy Lord and devote
thyself to Him with complete devotion.
*(Muzammil, 8)*

"You are also a sincere lover: listen to me with the ear
of your heart. There are four districts in this City of Love
and Inspiration to which you have come. These four districts are one within the other.

"The outer one is called *Muqallid*, the district of the
imitators. The skillful doctor you seek to cure your ills is
not within that district. Neither is the pharmacy that has
medicine for the sickness of heedlessness, darkness of the
heart, and hidden polytheism. Although you will find many
who advertise themselves as doctors of the heart —
appearing as such, dressing in robes, and wearing great
turbans; declaring themselves to be wise men while trying
to hide their ignorance, their depravity, their lack of character; unable to prove what they claim to be; seeking fame,
and ambitious for the world — they themselves are sick
with the sickness of themselves. They assign partners to
Allah, and are masters only of imitation.

"They hide their intrigue, duplicity, and malice well.
They are intelligent, perceptive, jolly and humorous, bon
vivant. Although their tongues appear to be pronouncing
the prayers and the names of Allah and you find them often
in the circles of dervishes, their minds, which guide them,
do not lead them to see the influence and benefit of their
prayers. Therefore you will not find with them the balm to
soothe the pains of unconsciousness and forgetfulness.

"You may as well leave this district of imitators and
take refuge in the district of *Mujahid*, the district of
warriors."

I followed his advice and went to the district of the warriors. The people I met there were weak and thin; gentle, thoughtful, thankful; devoted to praying, obeying, fasting, contemplating, and meditating. Their strength lay in living in accordance with that which they knew. I became close to them, and saw that they had left all the failures of character produced by egoism and egotism and the shadow of unconsciousness. They had formed a talent for being servants, pleased with their Lord and content with their state. I stayed in the district of the gentle warriors for many years. I acted as they acted and lived as they lived, seeing how I acted and how I lived, not letting a moment pass in heedlessness. I learned and showed patience and forbearance, and learned to be content and satisfied with my lot, and I was content and satisfied.

I fought hard, day and night, with my ego, but still I was left with the polytheism of many "me"s and "I"s fighting amongst themselves, even though they faced one Allah. This, my sickness of *shirk khafi* — setting up many "I"s as partners to Allah — cast heavy shadows over my heart, hid the truth, and kept me in heedlessness.

I asked the doctors of the district, I begged them. I told them of my sickness, the hidden polytheism, the awful heedlessness, the darkness of the heart, and asked for help. They told me, "Even in this place of those who battle their egos there is no cure for your ills, for

He is with you wherever you are."
(*Hadid*, 4)

Then they advised me to travel in the direction of the castle of *Mutma'ina*, the City of Peace and Tranquility. Near that city lay a district called *Munajaat wa Muraqaba* — supplication and meditation. Perchance there, they said, there would be a doctor to cure me.

When I came to the district of meditation I saw its inhabitants, quiet and peaceful, remembering Allah inwardly, reciting His Beautiful Names. To each and every one of them a son of the heart had been born. They stood, heads bowed in the presence of their Lord, silent, melancholic, sad, in deep humility and veneration. Although their exteriors seemed annihilated, ruinous, their hearts shone and flourished.

Their ways were gentle and courteous. They barely spoke with each other for fear of distracting each other's attention from the One in Whose presence they felt themselves to be, preventing each other from deep meditation. Light as feathers they were, yet they feared most to be a burden and a load on others.

I spent many years in the district of meditation and contemplation. I did as they did, and indeed I thought I was finally cured of heedlessness, polytheism, and unconsciousness. But I was not cured of the hidden dualism of "I" and "He" that still cast heavy shadows upon my heart.

My tears ran in torrents. Wretched and in total awe I fell into a strange state where an ocean of sadness surrounded me. I wished to drown in that sea. I found no other solution but to die. But I could not do anything, I had no will, not even to die.

As I stood there helpless, sad, in ecstasy, there appeared the beautiful teacher whom I had first met in these strange lands, the one who was called *Hidaya*, the Guide. He looked upon me with compassionate eyes. "O poor slave of himself, in exile in this foreign land! O wanderer away from home! O poor wretched one, you cannot find your cure in this state of spirit. Leave this place. Go to that district yonder, just next to the gate of the castle of *Mutma'ina*. The name of that quarter is *Fana* — self-annihilation. There you will find doctors who have annihilated their selves, who have no being, who know the secret of *fa-afnu thumma afnu thumma afnu fa-abku thumma abku thumma abku* — "Be nought, be nought, be nought, so that you will be, so that you will be, so that you will be forever."

Without delay, I went to the district of annihilation. I saw its population mute, speechless, as if dead, with no strength in them to utter a word. They had left the hope of any benefit from talk and were ready to give up their souls to the angel of death. They were totally unconcerned whether I was there or not.

I saw no action among them except their performing their prayers five times a day. They had lost the concept of separation between this world and the Hereafter, forgotten it. Pain and joy were equal to them. They had no taste for either material or spiritual things. No thought preoccupied them. They did not remember anything, nor did they look forward to anything. All need and desire was strange to them. They had even stopped asking Allah for what they wanted.

I stayed with them for many years. I did what they did. I did not appear other than they, but I did not know their inner state, so I could not do what they did inwardly.

Even in that place, among them, I felt great pain. Yet when I wished to describe the symptoms of my ill, I couldn't find a body nor any existence, so as to say "This is my body" or "This is me." Then I knew that which was "me," turned into the owner of me. Then I knew that to say "That being is mine" is a lie, and to lie is a sin for everyone. Then I knew that to ask the real owner for what was "mine" was the hidden polytheism of which I had wished to rid myself. What, then, was to be done?

In awe, I saw that I was free of all my wishes. I cried and cried. In my despair, if I were to call upon Him and say, "O Lord," then there would be two — I and He, me and the One from Whom I seek help, the will and the Willed, the desire and the Desired, the lover and the Beloved, oh so many. I knew not the remedy.

The woeful wailing attracted the pity of the angel of inspiration whom his Lord had charged to teach the lovers. With the permission of his Lord, he read to me from the book of divine inspiration: "First, annihilate your actions."

He gave that to me as a gift. As I stretched my hand to receive it, I saw that there was no hand. It was a composition of water and earth and ether and fire. I had no hand to take with. I had no power to act.

There is only One Who has power, the All-Powerful. Whatever action occurs through me, it belongs to the Absolute Actor. All power, all acts, I referred to Him, and I left all that happened to me and through me in this world. I knew, as I had been taught by the angel of inspiration, what the annihilation of one's actions is. And all praise is due to Allah.

The proof of the necessity of disowning one's actions in the path to truth is in the verse in the Holy Qur'an:

*Qul kullun min 'indilla-hi,*

Say, all [action] is from Allah.
*(An-Nisaa, 78)*

I am unlettered and have not been taught, yet Allah Most High in His manifestation of the Ultimate Truth has graced me with the ability and power to teach. As what is related here are occurrences that happened to me, experiences that brought a state of mind and spirit, and as it is said, *al-halu la yu'rafu bil-qal* — "the states cannot be told by words" — it is not possible to express such states so that others can appreciate or even imagine them.

Then I wished, with the permission of Allah and with the help of the angel of inspiration, to leave my attributes — those qualities which make one's personality. When I looked, what I saw was not mine. When I talked, what I said was not mine. Neither was the content mine. Totally helpless, I was cut off from all the attributes, visible and invisible, that distinguished me, from all qualities exterior and interior that had made me "me."

With all my being and feeling and spirit, I supposed myself a pure essence. Then I sensed that even this was duality. What do I have to do, what relation do I have, with something that does not belong to me? I was helpless again.

Then even my essence was taken away from me. Still I wished and longed for Him. I felt the meaning of

*wa talibu 'ayni 'abdi*

The one who longs for Me is My true servant.

Woe to this me in me, I know not what to do. Helpless, I hope for union.

*Wa Llahu bi kulli shay'in muhit,*

Allah Who

encompasses all things,

*huwal-awwalu wal-akhiru waz-zahiru wal-batinu
wa huwa bi kulli shay'in 'alim,*

Who is

before the before, and after the after, and all that
is evident and all that is hidden, and He is the
knower of all things became manifest in the
secret of my heart.

Even then I wished that the secret of *mutu qabla an tamu-tu*, "to die before dying," be actualized in me. O woe, again this hidden duality of I and the One I long for. This, too, cannot be the truth.

What ill is this that gives pangs of pain when I move, when I wish, when I long, when I ask for help, when I pray and beg? What strange state have I fallen into, difficult to resolve?

Helpless, I gave all these to their Owner and waited at the gate of acquiescence in agony of death, senseless, without thought or feeling, as if dead, expecting death to take me at every breath. I stayed in that state I know not how long.

Following the advice *istafid qalbaka* — "Ask your heart," I told my heart to instruct me. It said, "As long as there is a trace of you in you, you cannot hear your Lord's call *irji'* — '*Come to Me!*' "

If a cat fell into a salt pit and drowned, and in time its body became salt, if a single hair were left, could that salt be used as food? How often and how long do theologians debate and discuss such matters! Some say that in spite of the single hair the salt is clean, that the corpse of the cat is now the salt; and some say that the single hair is as much as the cat as was the whole body. Thus the salt is dirty and unlawful to eat.

I felt the truth of it and wished that trace of me in me would die. I immersed that trace in divine beatitude. An ecstasy came, from me, to me, over that which was mine, covering it all, the taste of which is impossible to describe. Without ear, without words, without letters I heard the invitation: *Irji'* — *"Come."*

I tried to think, "What is this state?" My thought could not think it. I was made to know that thought cannot think about the sacred secret. Even that knowledge was taken away from me as fast as it came to me.

O seeker, what has been said here is not intended to show that I know. Therefore it will only be made known to you after I am gone from among you. It is for the benefit of the seekers of truth, for the lovers who long for the Beloved, so that it may help them to know themselves, so that they may find in which of the cities I traveled through they themselves are, and which of its citizens they befriend. When and if in sincerity they know their place, they will act accordingly, and know the direction of the gate of Allah's pleasure, and be thankful. Perchance they will remember this *faqir*, the writer of these words, with a little prayer.

*Allah's peace and blessings be upon Shaykh Muhammad Sadiq Naqshbandi Erzinjani, the original writer of these words, and the ones who read them. Al-Fatihah.*